TAKING NOTE

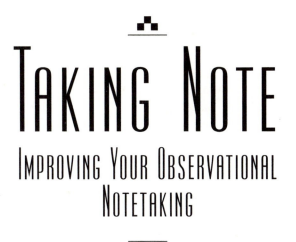

TAKING NOTE

IMPROVING YOUR OBSERVATIONAL NOTETAKING

BRENDA MILLER POWER

STENHOUSE PUBLISHERS
PORTLAND, MAINE

Stenhouse Publishers

Library of Congress Cataloging-in-Publication Data
Power, Brenda Miller.
    Taking note : improving your observational notetaking / Brenda Miller Power.
      p. cm.
    Includes bibliographical references (p.).
    ISBN 1-57110-035-0 (alk. paper)
    1. Students—Rating of—United States.   2. Note-taking.
    3. Observation (Eduational method)   I. Title.
    LB3051.P617   1996
    371.2'7—dc20   96-28319
                                          CIP

Cover and interior design by Catherine Hawkes
Cover photo by Andrew Edgar
Typeset by Technologies 'N Typography, Inc.
Manufactured in the United States of America on acid-free paper
05   9 8 7 6 5

To those who take care of the daily details, especially
Susan Russell and Martha Pojasek

CONTENTS

1 ◆ Introduction: Living a Balanced Life

I have the most wonderful job in the world. I teach teachers—mostly about literacy, but lately about many other things too. There has never been a better or more challenging time to be a teacher.

Probably one of the most exciting areas of change in literacy involves research and assessment of students. Teachers are learning to be careful observers of their students. Through daily and systematic recording of what children do in the classroom, educators are able to plan thoughtful and relevant instruction.

At least that's our ideal, isn't it? But for every teacher who fits this ideal, with assessment portfolios and research notebooks neatly lining the walls of the classroom, folders bulging with information about students, there are a few dozen others who fall far short of this vision. For us, it feels like it's time to write another assessment every time we blink our bleary eyes. Each September we start with a clear desk and clear head, with fresh plans for notes and observations. By late October, these plans are buried under the flurry of work that must be done.

This is a handbook for the well-intentioned but overwhelmed teacher. If you are someone who reads and admires the work of teacher researchers and colleagues who keep careful notes on student learning, but you have no idea where to begin in tackling the mound of work before you, this book is for you.

I wrote this handbook because it is something I wish I had had in my own teaching life ten years ago. When I first began to work with teachers, I was single, with few relationships outside those with my teaching and graduate school classmates. I became obsessive about my work. I was eating, living, and breathing literacy theory and practice. There weren't enough hours in the day (or at night) to write, talk, and argue literacy ideals with teachers. I was pals with the janitors at the schools I worked in because I usually arrived at first light and left after dark. I don't regret those early days of total immersion in my field. I don't think I've ever been as inspired or energized by ideas since.

But my life changed. I married a man who doesn't know the difference between a diphthong and a dipstick (I consider this an asset). Eventually, I became a parent. Over time, I realized that there honestly aren't enough hours in the day to lead two lives—one as an obsessive literacy advocate, the other as a committed family caregiver. I had to find ways to live one balanced life, moving between these worlds.

This handbook is not the work of a superteacher. It is a handbook filled with the stories of teachers who admire those superteachers but find they must adapt the work of their heros and heroines to the constraints of their own lives. The strategies in this handbook will help you learn how to take notes more carefully and systematically in your classroom and write narratives about students without making too many sacrifices in other areas of your life.

MAKING THE IDEAL REAL

The strategies in this handbook are an outgrowth of the work I have done over the past twelve years with teachers at every grade level who are trying to do research in their classrooms and assess their students. I am also a teacher researcher, and I don't suggest anything I haven't tried with my own students. In my work with teachers, I try to help them see how notetaking and observation of students can be a natural part of the somewhat unnatural lives we teachers lead. The Maine teachers I work with are famed for their straightforward nature and straight talk. They are eager to try new things but also quite blunt if they think an idea or technique is too idealistic or too far removed from the reality of their lives in the classroom. We share a common goal—we work together to build systematic profiles of learners at all levels and to build curricula from what we are seeing in our classrooms.

As I've continued to work with teachers over the years, I've realized that for many of us, an even more important goal rests just beneath the surface of what we talk about. These teachers are graduate students, and they have spent the past few years moving from classroom to home to graduate school to professional meetings, without many spare moments in their days. Like I was at the start of my career, many of these teachers are obsessive in their work. I've come to see that part of my job is to work with teachers to find ways to do our job well and still find time for life beyond the classroom, whatever that life may be.

Ticked Off at Checklists

I think this quest for balance in teaching, assessment, and life is what has led to the blizzard of literacy assessment checklists in the past decade. One week in a graduate assessment class I taught, we compiled as many literacy assessment checklists as we could find just to get a sense of how many were out there. We found more than 150 different forms.

This search for the ideal checklist or assessment chart has been the Holy Grail of the literacy field for too long now, and it needs to end. If you've tried any checklists lately, I suspect you've reached the same conclusion as we have: checklists don't work if your goal is to give a rich portrait of individual children. If a checklist does miraculously have many of the developmental milestones appropriate for the children you work with, then it is too unwieldy to work with. The shorter checklists usually work for a small number of children in any class. But too many students are far past the skills on any list in their abilities, and too many have too far to go to reach the beginning threshold of skills presented. That's the reality of life in classrooms.

It's not surprising that teachers resist the clearly superior alternative to checklists narrative assessments. Who has time for all the notetaking, observing, and drafting of narratives? There is no time built into the school day for this work, and so we continue to refine, restructure, and rebuild checklists and report cards that we know don't begin to fit our conception of what assessments should look like.

If you are a conscientious teacher, there is a good chance you are also a teacher who is overwhelmed. I have written this handbook not as a plea for you to give more time that you don't have to observing and writing about your students. I want this handbook to help you find more time for the things you care about (in and out of the classroom) and still find time to write more cogent and thoughtful notes and narratives about your students. I hope it helps you shift the ways you use the time you have.

I've organized this handbook around a series of principles that can help you learn to keep better observational records of your students. Each chapter outlines different principles around one specific topic and ends with a series of activities you can do alone or with colleagues to help you apply those principles in your teaching life.

There are all kinds of ways to use this handbook. You might want to read straight through and pick just a few activities or strategies to try randomly. You may want to enlist a colleague to go step-by-step through the handbook and try each of the suggestions with you. The handbook is a good starting point for whole school faculties who are considering trying narrative assessments or teacher-research projects together but lack some basic knowledge in how to take the notes that are essential components of these new initiatives.

No one needs more work—so make this handbook work for you. And the first step, regardless of how you'll use this book, is defining some of the work you do now and how you do it.

Getting Started

1. Try to find at least one friend or colleague willing to do the activities in this handbook with you.

It's possible to do the activities in this handbook on your own—many teachers have done so and learned a lot from them. But they often work best if you have a partner to cajole, nag, support, and encourage you when you need it. The colleague needn't be in the same school or even the same town, but you will need some support to make changes in your teaching and assessment.

Set aside one hour per week to meet or talk on the phone about the activities in the handbook. It's helpful to list the actual times these conferences will occur for the first three weeks you are working together. Whether it's one person or a dozen, support helps if you are going to make substantial changes in your classroom notetaking.

2. Buy a small notebook, stenographer's pad, or calendar diary.

For one week, keep track of how you spend your time in the classroom. You might choose to do this record keeping during writer's workshop or while children are working quietly or independently in groups.

These notes can be very rough. What you're looking for are patterns.

- What surprises you about the way you spend your time?

- What takes up the bulk of your time?

- What took more time than you expected?

- What took less time than you expected?

- Where could or should cuts in your use of time be made?

At the end of the week, look at the allocation of time and brainstorm strategies for finding more time for notetaking. These strategies might include ways of encouraging students to interrupt you less, giving children more responsibility for classroom tasks, or having students lead whole class discussions to enable you to sit back and record observations.

3. Take no work home for a week.

This may seem like the most crazy and difficult beginning task for many readers, so don't worry if you just can't accomplish it. But I encourage you to try, especially if the end of every day involves packing up loads of materials to bring home.

This handbook is about breaking habits. After one week, you will be free to lug home wheelbarrels if it works for you. But for one week, try to experience what it is like to have all your work accomplished within school walls. This might mean you have to double up on work the week before you make this commitment. You may have to have students respond to each other's work for a week, rather than relying on your response. You may have to go to school an hour early and leave an hour later than usual. All this will take planning and commitment—car-pool and day-care arrangements might need to be made, explanations will have to be made for curricular changes.

When teachers don't bring work home for a week, they are amazed at how strange and wonderful it feels. A colleague exclaimed, "It feels like I'm missing a limb or something every afternoon as I drive home!" Another teacher expressed a common sentiment, "It's made me realize how sloppy I've become in my work. Lord knows, I don't get to even a fraction of the papers and professional books I lug home every night. I've just grown accustomed to hauling this stuff around. I'm thinking more about what each evening really will look like and whether or not there should be a place for work in it."

Try it—you'll be amazed at how light it makes you feel. Some teachers have even discovered with delight that they have a spouse buried under a pile of newspapers on the couch.

4. At the end of the first week, take a critical look at your time log.

Develop three strategies to try in your classroom to buy yourself back some time. If you've found a colleague to work with, talk together about the experience of not bringing work home. If you did find yourself sneaking out one afternoon with a small tote bag or file folder, 'fess up. Examine why it's so hard to make your work fit into working hours and what this might mean if you're going to make changes in the way you take notes about your students.

My strategies for getting more time for notetaking in the classroom:

1. _____

_____

_____

2. _____

_____

_____

3. _____

_____

_____

2 Taking Stock and Setting Goals

I love cookbooks. I have an entire brass bookshelf on one wall of my kitchen filled with plants and cookbooks on every imaginable cuisine. But I don't cook much. My husband just rolls his eyes when I enter the house with a new cookbook in one hand and a box of Chinese takeout in the other. I love the idea of cooking more than the reality. It's very hard for me to move from the bookshelf to the stove.

Notetaking and what it leads to for teachers—research projects and narrative assessments of students—can be like my love of cookbooks. I love the idea of bringing together all the food ingredients as a personal and creative expression of caregiving in my home. But I always seem to find a reason—a lacking ingredient or two (ginger? time?)— that keeps me from the daily habit of home-cooked meals.

This section of the handbook is going to help you determine some of those "few missing ingredients" in your teaching life that stop your own move from the bookshelf to the stove when it comes to careful notetaking. If you're going to get cooking with notetaking, you're going to need to take stock of what's already in place in your classroom when it comes to notetaking and student responsibilities. This is the time when you have to clean out a few cupboards, so to speak, and reorganize to make room for testing out some new notetaking strategies.

I'm not going to start by making a case for the value of good notetaking practices for research and assessment. When the teachers I work with make a list of what they are tired of in the books they read, being preached at is at the top of the list. They know what they are supposed to do—they just don't have a good sense of where to begin to restructure their lives and teaching days to make all the changes they know are needed.

The Retrospective Curriculum

If you are reading this handbook, chances are you're pretty savvy about recent changes in education theory and practice. You've probably already decided that mandated, prefabricated curricula won't work in your classroom. The way to find out what does work is to document what is happening in our classrooms and learn from what we see. This "retrospective" curriculum becomes the basis of what we do in the future, and it's a never-ending cycle of initiation, reflection, and change. Teachers want to create portraits of children—in research, in the assessments that go into permanent files, in conferences with parents— that truly show who that child is and how she is unique.

Notes keep you focused on the part of your job that really matters—your students and learning. By observing your classroom closely and slowly compiling information about students and your curriculum over time, you build your own confidence in what you are doing. Teachers who keep good notes on student achievement and their curriculum are usually confident teachers.

It's getting into that cycle of initiation, reflection, and change and out of the grind—of forms to fill out, discipline to mete out, and always, paper to deal with—that this book can help with. Now that you've had your first taste of breaking a habit by not taking work home for a week, it's time to look at the classroom habits that keep you out of that cycle of initiation, reflection, and change.

It's not the hours that add up—it's the minutes. Five minutes here, ten minutes there, and soon there's no time at all for the reflection that is at the heart of good notetaking and teaching.

During my first ten years of teaching, I usually collected a set of some sort of papers from students each class period. At some point before the next class period, I would spend ten to fifteen minutes writing down who turned in what that day. It wasn't much time, just an hour or two a week. But I added an hour or two each week times forty weeks of the year, times ten years; I realized I had spent *over 600* hours keeping records my students could easily keep themselves.

Now when I enter my college classroom I carry a three-ring binder with pockets. Students sign up for chores every other week—anything from opening the class with a reading to picking up the AV equipment we will need from the central supply area. One of the chores is to keep the class records. One student circulates through the room early in the class period, determining who has completed their work. I explain the chore to the first student who signs up on the first day in September. After that, new class recorders are always trained by the previous recorder. It is never my responsibility again.

Another chore students sign up for is class historian. In the middle of the folder is loose-leaf paper for the class history. The class historian writes a one-page record of what we did that day in class. It includes the things I planned to do—the workshops, presentations, videotapes. But it also includes the daily surprises—the unexpected comment that led to a half-hour discussion of tracking, the opening or closing reading by a student that had classmates doubled over in laughter. This class history by students is much more detailed than the notes I used to keep of what happened in each class. Because they keep such a good record of the details of our whole class experience, I have more time to think and write about individual students. And I have more material—both from the whole class and from my individual observations—to use in my assessments and research.

I encouraged you in the first part of the book to break habits outside of school—by meeting regularly with colleagues about notetaking and by not taking work home. You've also begun to think in broad terms about the uses of time in your classroom and to consider where changes are possible. Now it's time to think specifically about forming notetaking habits.

Sharing the Responsibility of Notetaking

The best teachers I know are very good at sharing responsibilities with students, parents, and colleagues. I know, I know—you already do this. Every good teacher does. I don't enter many classrooms now where students don't have responsibilities like attendance and calendar duties each day. But if you're like me, there are still small pockets of time each day when you do chores that students could easily handle. Is there a way to add a class historian chore to some parts of the day? Could students keep some class records you keep now or add to the records you already have? In Jane Doan and Penny Chase's multiage K–2 class in Benton, Maine, one child is responsible for taking notes during the morning message period. This is a time when children read and respond to a message written by one of the teachers. While one teacher leads, the other takes notes alongside the designated student notetaker. Even the very youngest children find ways to represent what they see (see Figure 2.1). These records say a lot about both the recorder and recordee.

But the most amazing example of Jane and Penny's record keeping takes place outside the classroom. After I visited Jane and Penny's class a few times, I got the nagging feeling something was missing in the mornings. I finally figured out what it was. No matter what day I visited, I never saw lunch money being counted. It was then I discovered that the *bus drivers* are responsible for counting and turning in lunch money.

The system works beautifully. It's a large consolidated school of almost eight hundred students, with nearly every child bused to school. Bus drivers quickly get a sense of which children are likely to forget their lunch money, and are apt to send those children back into the house for it on Monday before they even get on the bus. Children who

FIGURE 2.1   Sample Notetaking of Five-Year-Olds in Jane Doan and Penny Chase's Classroom

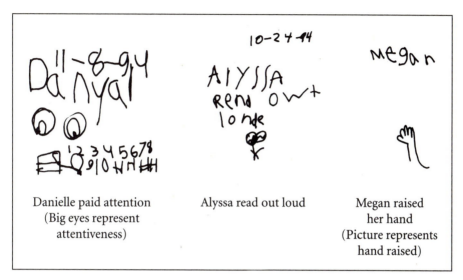

Danielle paid attention (Big eyes represent attentiveness)

Alyssa read out loud

Megan raised her hand (Picture represents hand raised)

do forget their money head right to the lunchroom to make arrangements with the cafeteria staff. Imagine the thousands of hours classroom teachers in this school have for other tasks because they are not responsible for lunch-money records!

You need to do a bit of weeding and sorting, looking for ways you can reorganize your notetaking and enlist the help of others. If you don't find those pockets of time for new responsibilities, any insights from this handbook will soon be lost as you fall back into old habits.

GETTING FOCUSED

Make a List of All the Records You Keep Now

Most important, think about why you keep them. How often do you take them? How often do you refer back to them? What are they for? Could anyone else keep these records? (See Figure 2.2.)

Figure 2.2   Record Worksheet

Record	How often do I keep it? (daily, weekly, sporadically)	What is it for?	Could someone else keep it? (student, parent, aide) Could it be eliminated?
1.			
2.			
3.			
4.			
5.			
6.			
7.			
8.			
9.			
10.			
11.			
12.			
13.			
14.			
15.			
16.			

Set a Goal for Improving Your Notetaking

You need to figure out how to make this handbook work for you. What is your goal? How is it different from the goals of your colleagues who are working with you? The more specific and concrete you can be, the more you will learn from this handbook.

For example, you may want to write narratives to attach to the report cards your school requires. If you are writing individual narratives for a whole class of students, this will mean fewer notes about the class as a whole and a system that ensures all students have at least a few notes about their work each quarter. Or you may want to take a more active role in consultations with specialists over your students. Or there may just be a few students you have trouble understanding in your class and you may limit your notetaking to just these few students.

Some readers may just want to get a handle on the notes they take already. If the informal assessments you do now seem random and unfocused, you may want to set a goal of getting more organized in your notes—weeding out the kinds of records that don't serve you and your students well, and adding a few notetaking strategies that maximize your time.

Take just a few minutes to prioritize your notetaking goals (see the checklist on the next page).

The most important goal I have is:

_____

_____

_____

_____

Why is this goal important to me?

_____

_____

_____

_____

What might get in the way of my accomplishing this goal?

_____

_____

_____

_____

How can my colleagues help me overcome these obstacles?

_____

_____

_____

_____

3 TOOLS OF THE TRADE

Sometimes nothing makes you feel more like a professional than having the right tools. My sister, Mary Stein, is a science education professor. She shows teachers how they can build a science program out of saved mayonnaise jars and discarded paper-towel rolls. Mary says science is the stuff of everyday life, and that can be reflected in the tools we use to "do science."

At the same time, she argues that teachers and students need test tubes, balance scales, and Bunsen burners. Scientists use specific tools. And part of becoming a scientist is having the right tools to do your work.

Teachers observing students need tools, too. You certainly don't need many—some people would argue that the pad of paper on your desk and the pen in your hand is enough. But teachers I've worked with have found they usually need to experiment with different materials to find what works best for them as they observe and write about their students. Having a variety of materials at your disposal will enable you to try a variety of strategies for observing in your classroom. There isn't one right way to observe students. Testing out a variety of notetaking materials can help you find the right way for you.

A Shopping List

You'll want to schedule some time alone or with your research partner to wander the aisles of an office supply store for notetaking materials. Some of these may already be available at your school, or you might want to add them to your supply requests at the start of the school year. Most are quite inexpensive.

Address Labels

Buy the plain white variety with adhesive on the back, in a variety of sizes (1-by-3-inch up to 3-by-4-inch). You'll also want some colored-coded labels—these have a thin line of red, yellow, blue, or green at the top.

Post-its

You'll want standard sizes in a variety of colors.

Post-it Flags

A new item, enabling you to tab your notes and easily move the tabs as you look at different issues in your classroom. You'll want a variety of colors for highlighting different points. These flags come in a number of styles, with many including space for notes on the flag.

Label Dots

These are small colored dots of different sizes. Buy the smallest—they are useful for coding your observations later in the process.

Carbon Paper

A lost treasure! The new varieties don't smear like those from our youth. Carbon paper is great if you have a school where Attila the Hun guards the copy machine. Often you'll need only one copy of your notes in your assessment or research, and using carbon paper regularly can save lots of organization time, energy, and expense.

Loose-leaf Paper

You know what you like—lined or unlined. You'll want paper that is punched for three-ring binders. If you have previously used only lined paper, make sure you purchase some unlined, and vice versa. This will help you see new possibilities for your notetaking.

There are also new papers that are lined and have a wide left margin. This "project planner" paper, often found in notebooks, is perfect for taking "notes on notes" after you've done your initial observations (see Figure 3.1).

Pens or Pencils

Get a supply of your favorite pens or pencils—splurge and buy the best. It will help you get in the mood for taking notes. You'll also want to buy highlighting pens in a few different colors (pink, blue, yellow).

Smock or Large Pocket Notebook

Many teachers like to have a smock with many pockets to house all their notetaking supplies. Having a smock you put on when you're ready to write observations is a great physical reminder that you'll be concentrating on notetaking for the next ten minutes or hour. If you buy a smock, load it up with a variety of the supplies you have purchased—address labels of various sizes, Post-its, pens and pencils.

If you've never been a person who enjoys dress-up, you might

FIGURE 3.1   Project Planner Paper

PAGE NUMBER	DATE	
	/ /	
PROJECT		

COMMENTS	ACTIONS/TASKS
	1
	2
	3
	4
	5
	6
	7
	8
	9
	10
	11
	12
	13
	14
	15
	16
	17
	18
	19
	20
	21
	22
	23
	24
	25
	26
	27
	28

prefer the more sedate large pocket notebook. This notebook, like the smock, should be loaded to the gills with your supplies. After a few weeks, you'll get a sense of what supplies you aren't using much. These can go in the back of the notebook. But try to keep at least a sample of most of the supplies I've listed here somewhere in your smock or notebook. When you get stuck in your notetaking or stymied by your system, just the presence of different supplies can point to alternative ways of organizing your work.

If you have a larger budget, there are three expensive items to add to your wish list.

Laptop Computer

Great for taking notes while students are interacting, and it gives you a leg up on writing narratives because you already have information in the computer.

Transcribing Machine

If any of your assessments involve tape-recording, transcribing machines can cut your transcription time by 50 percent. These are modified tape recorders that allow you to vary the speed of the tape through foot pedals and automatically back up the tape a bit every time you stop the tape while transcribing. Many teachers who do regular interviews with students wonder how they survived without these machines once they try them out.

Small Photocopier

Photocopiers that are quite rudimentary, allowing only a set number of copies to be made per month, are often adequate for a classroom, especially if you are using them solely to enhance and develop your observation and notetaking program. Providing students with a copy of your notes at the same time you put the notes into your assessment or research log will prove extremely beneficial to students and will save you loads of time later.

The last three items are drastically reduced in price if you buy used goods. Often the best place to start looking is university or office surplus stores. Many computer stores sell used equipment, and no technology is evolving faster than laptop computers. This means you can get a good model, used little, for a fraction of the cost of new models. Many of these used machines have more capability than you would ever need for notetaking. It might be possible to pool resources and share a laptop with your colleagues.

New transcribing machines can often cost four hundred dollars. I purchased eight perfectly fine used machines for twenty-five dollars each last year from my university surplus department, and I loan these out to teachers regularly. Transcribing machines are often purchased for one specific research project at a university, and they used to be standard equipment for secretaries. When the research project is ended, or the vice president stops dictating memos, the transcriber sits in a closet gathering dust. If you live anywhere near a college or university, call the surplus office to see how they advertise equipment for sale. The same is true for small copy machines—offices are always upgrading their equipment, and often these used machines have been very well-maintained.

MAKING THE TOOLS WORK FOR YOU

Once you have your new notetaking materials spread in front of you, you can begin to think about new possibilities for observing students. Go back to the records you keep now. Is there a way to color code your observations to save time and simplify your system? For example, if you decide to use only pink Post-its for reading observations, yellow for writing workshop, and green for science, you'll know immediately what aspect of the curriculum the observation refers to.

If you haven't used carbon paper recently, you'll wonder how you lived without it. For example, if you have the best intentions of regularly photocopying your notes from whole class discussions of a student's work but rarely find time to run to the machine, perhaps you can insert a piece of carbon paper under your recording sheet, enabling you immediately to give a copy of your notes to the student as the class discussion ends.

This technique can also work for managing whole class or individual student records. If you write observations of individual students on address labels in a running column with carbon underneath, you can have a copy of your notes for whole class assessments, research, and discussion (see Figure 3.2). The original address labels can be placed in individual student folders, according to whom they refer.

Depending upon the age of your students and the records they keep, you may want them to experiment with these supplies, too.

Project planner paper is a great tool for collective student/teacher notes. If you assign a student to serve each day as the class historian, he or she can note what takes place in class that day on the right-hand side of the page. This leaves room for you to write your notes (daily or weekly) in the left-hand column (see Figure 3.3). I've found dozens of uses for this paper since discovering it two years ago.

You won't really know the best uses of these supplies till after you've actually begun to do observations and take notes in new ways. But you can brainstorm some uses based upon the records you already keep.

You may want to try out the same new tool or strategy with your team or colleague to get their ideas about how you can adapt the tool to meet your needs and those of your students. This is a time to play with the materials, feeling free to use what works and discard (at least for now) what doesn't (see the checklist on page 26).

FIGURE 3.2   Labels and Carbon Paper

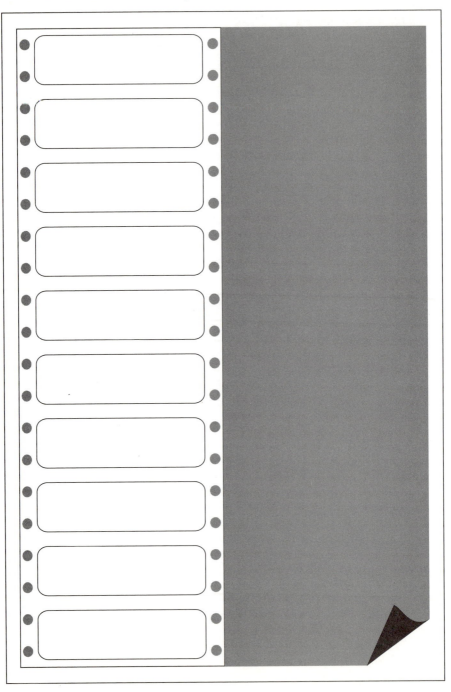

FIGURE 3.3 Project Planner Paper Is a Great Tool for Collective Student/Teacher Notes

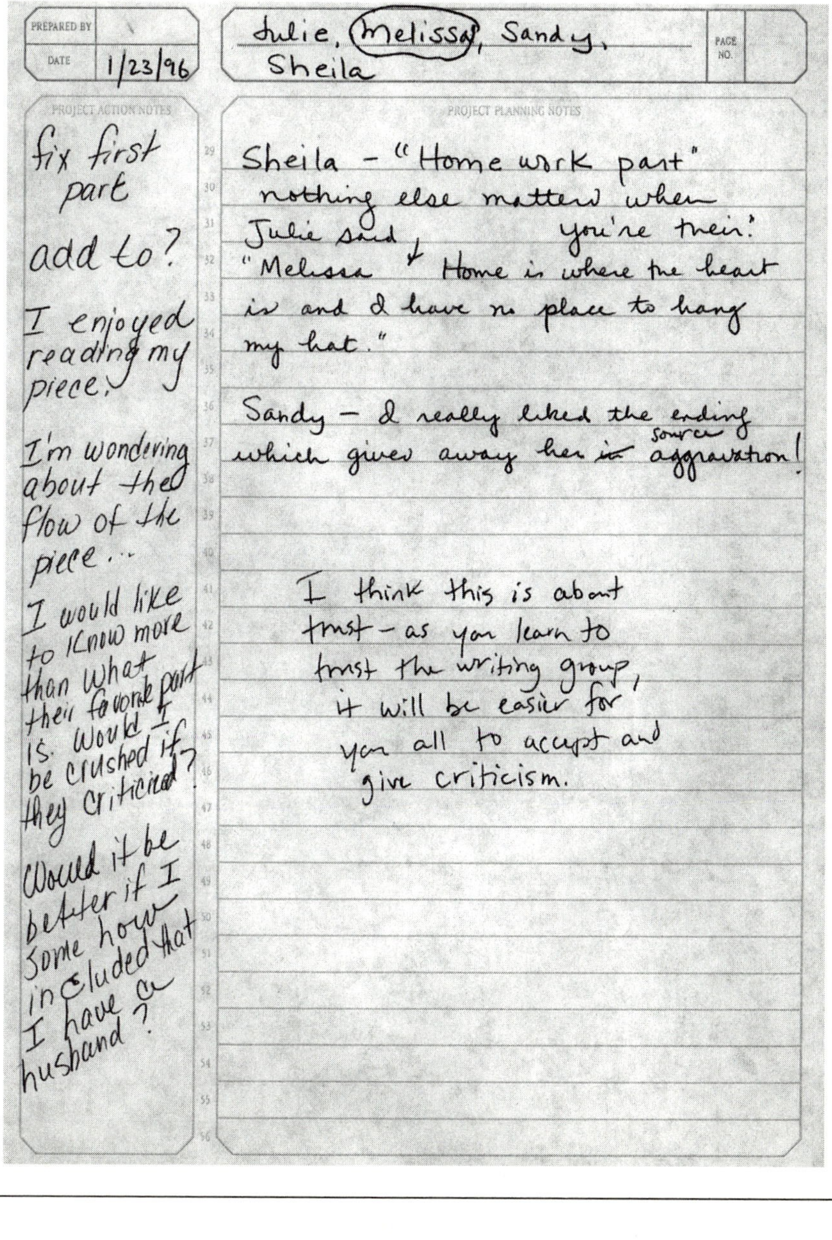

PREPARED BY

DATE 1/23/96

Julie, Melissa, Sandy, Sheila

PAGE NO.

PROJECT ACTION NOTES

fix first part

add to?

I enjoyed reading my piece.

I'm wondering about the flow of the piece...

I would like to know more than what their favorite part is. Would I be crushed if they criticized?

Would it be better if I somehow included that I have a husband?

PROJECT PLANNING NOTES

Sheila – "Home work part" nothing else mattered when Julie said, you're there.

"Melissa + Home is where the heart is and I have no place to hang my hat."

Sandy – I really liked the ending which gives away her ~~is~~ source aggravation!

I think this is about trust – as you learn to trust the writing group, it will be easier for you all to accept and give criticism.

1. Tool

_____

How I Will Use It

_____

How Will This Improve My Teaching or Record Keeping?

_____

2. Tool

_____

How I Will Use It

_____

How Will This Improve My Teaching or Record Keeping?

_____

3. Tool

_____

How I Will Use It

_____

How Will This Improve My Teaching or Record Keeping?

_____

4 WHEN TO WRITE

*Memory is made as a quilt
is made. From the whole
cloth of time, frayed scraps
of sensation are pulled apart
and pieced together in a
pattern that has a name.*

Kim Stafford

When you write will determine what you write. From the whole cloth of everything that occurs in your classroom, you will need to decide what story or stories need to be told and when it most makes sense to gather together the pieces of what you see, hear, and feel to tell that story. Determining when to take notes means you'll have to consider many factors—your personality as a teacher, the needs of your students, and the goals for your notes.

Regardless of what the story will be, there are two times observational notes can be taken: "in the midst" and "after the fact." It's helpful if you think about and test out each way of taking notes as you begin to get into a rhythm and routine of observations. You need to figure out when notetaking makes the most sense in your classroom, fitting both your goals and the needs of the students.

"In the Midst" Notes

"In the midst" notes are the observations you make while your students are at work. You might write "in the midst" while walking through the room, with your notepad in hand or smock on, jotting down what you see. The writing might be on Post-its, address labels, or one side of a journal page.

If you're trying to find a time when it would make sense for you to take notes, consider those times when you want students to pay less attention to you and more attention to each other. In Pat McLure's multiage primary classroom, Pat takes notes during two components of her literacy program. She writes notes from the back of the room when children sit in the author's chair to read their writing to the whole class. This teaches them to focus attention on the writer in the chair, not on their teacher. Pat will still make comments and redirect the group if needed, but the notetaking serves the dual purpose of being a tool for assessing the group and a means to focus the group on the student writer and writing, not on Pat.

The other time Pat takes notes is during student literature discussion groups. Pat is always present when these groups of four meet. Once again, because some of her time is focused on notetaking, children attend to each other and the books more than they do to their teacher.

Pat has another, more subtle goal in taking these notes during whole class and small group discussion periods. When she meets with parents for assessment conferences, she can highlight how individual children are working within the class community. These notes reflect the value she places on individuals within the community, rather than focusing on individual achievement.

Many teachers choose to do their "in the midst" notes with just the opposite purpose. Clipboard in hand, they move through the classroom, conferencing with individual students. This has become all but standard procedure for notetaking during workshops, and I think it's one of the reasons teachers get frustrated with keeping anecdotal records and often stop doing it. When you're in a one-on-one conference with a student, it's distracting and time-consuming to stop and take notes about what happened in the conference. There is a rhythm you establish in moving among your students and an intensity in those individual conferences that is rarely matched in any other part of the curriculum. You are trying to listen intensely to one student while continually surveying what is happening in the rest of the room. Adding notetaking to that delicate mix of close attention and rapid, repeated scanning of the room is just too much for most teachers. Taking notes in the midst of students discussing their writing or literature, with their attention focused on each other, is much more manageable.

"AFTER THE FACT" NOTES

"After the fact" notes are made when students aren't present. You might choose to write in the quiet of your classroom early in the morning before students arrive, or at home in the journal you keep on your bedstand to write in just before you fall asleep. You might jot down notes on address labels while eating your lunch.

The benefits to writing "after the fact" are numerous. You can choose a quiet time without the distractions that are always present when you're working with students. What bubbles up in your mind when you are alone, away from students, are likely to be the most important events that happened that day in your classroom. The writing has more of a narrative flow—"after the fact" notes tend to be full sentences, while "in the midst" notes are generally brief, choppy words and phrases.

But there are also many drawbacks to writing "after the fact." The first is obvious. Teachers are not often successful at preserving pockets of time for work that doesn't absolutely need to be done. If you rarely find time for a bathroom break in the morning, it's hard to believe you'll be able consistently to carve out fifteen minutes of writing while your students are in morning recess.

I find it's best for me to take "after the fact" notes, and I do manage to keep to my routine even though I face the same distractions as any teacher. I meet with students for only three hours a week in each of my college classes, and there isn't a pocket of time in any of those hours when I would be comfortable taking notes. So I write for fifteen minutes after each class. I've found the only way I could develop this habit was to set some artificial rules and limits on myself.

I make myself remain in the classroom. This is important, because just being in the same physical space where I met with students sparks memories of events that occurred. I jot my notes on loose-leaf paper as I write responses to the in-class journals my students have written that day. It usually takes me no more than fifteen minutes to jot my notes, and at most another fifteen minutes to finish responses to those in-class journals.

The good thing about staying in the classroom is that it strictly limits the time I write in my teaching log and respond to student logs. Another class always comes in within a half hour during the day, and after evening classes I'm anxious to get home. When I'm sitting in the classroom, it's a quiet time, and it's easy to reflect on my teaching, but I also can feel the clock ticking.

Either "in the midst" or "after the fact" can be effective times for taking notes, depending upon how you work. And as you take notes, you'll find there are fewer boundaries between the two. As you sit in the back of the classroom, jotting down notes during whole class writing discussions, it's likely you'll make a note or two about something that was said an hour earlier as you circulated during writing conferences.

ESTABLISHING A ROUTINE

Once you decide when you're going to write, you'll need to find ways to preserve that time. This is no small feat for teachers. We want to capitalize on the teachable moments in our classroom, which means it's often hard to stick to routines. And unfortunately, others rarely see teachers' time as our own. Administrators cavalierly interrupt class schedules with assemblies featuring a talking moose droning on about dental hygiene; colleagues stop in for a quick cup of coffee during the time they know your students are in music class; a parent can only come in for a conference during a time outside the designated conference period.

With that in mind, the following activities can help you take tentative steps toward establishing some boundaries around the time you set for taking notes and observing students.

1. Link when you take notes to your goals.
Look back at the goals you listed for yourself in Chapter 2. What time or times of the day make the most sense for you to take notes to meet these goals? List both potential times for notetaking and reasons why notetaking during this time is linked to your goal. Try to list a few times when you might take notes in your classroom.

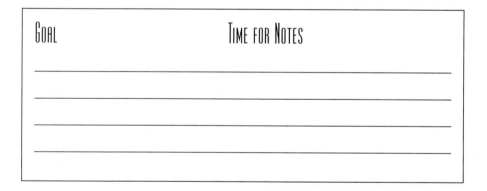

Goal	Time for Notes

2. Experiment with "In the Midst" and "After the Fact" notes.
Before you try to lock into a routine of notetaking, test out the different times of day you listed for these notes. This may take a few days or a few weeks, but you'll want to explore which times of day and kinds of notes work best for your needs.

As you test out different times for taking notes, don't worry much about what you write. Think instead of whether or not you are able to take notes consistently during these times. After at least a few days of trying to observe and write about students during different times, ask yourself, What period was most comfortable for me to take notes? What might get in the way of me consistently taking notes during this time?

3. Initiate a ritual.

Poet Georgia Heard writes, "Where I write, and the rituals I create for myself there, are crucial for keeping the writing spirit alive in me" (1989, 126). If you want to sustain the spirit of an active, questioning observer of your students, consider developing a few rituals that create a psychic "space" around the time you reserve for your notetaking. It might be putting on your smock when it's time for your fifteen minutes of notes; it might be moving to your desk to pull out your treasured favorite pen reserved only for your notes (and returning it to that spot after the notes are finished); it might be sitting for a couple of minutes at the rug area in your classroom as students go about their work, and thinking about what you'll write. My ritual of writing briefly after my students have left is so ingrained that I really can't leave the classroom until I've finished jotting down notes—my teaching feels incomplete without it.

Think about what rituals might work for you. Is there a hat or scarf you might put on to let students know you aren't to be disturbed as you're writing? Is there a sign that needs to be posted on your door during a planning period, to let colleagues know only emergencies warrant a disruption?

Take a moment to list one or two rituals you could institute to encourage consistency in your notetaking routine:

MY RITUALS

1._____

_____

_____

2._____

_____

_____

4. Let colleagues and students in on your work.
If students and colleagues know you value the time you put into your notetaking, they will help you protect that time. Enlist the people who might infringe upon your notetaking as allies, carefully explaining the purposes of your notetaking. Once they understand why you need to protect this time, some students and colleagues will become protective of your notetaking routine. As you're beginning to establish the notetaking routine in your classroom, you'll also want to schedule at least a small number of class discussions explaining why you'll need time for notes and how these notes will be helpful to the classroom community.

5. Save a small amount of time each week to look at all your notes from the week.
Set aside just a half hour or so in the early weeks of your notetaking to look over what you've written and flesh it out. You can encourage yourself to do this by using project planner paper, which provides you with that extra margin for additional jottings. At least a small part of the time you schedule for your notes needs to be for this reflection and clean-up. If possible, schedule this time with a colleague and talk together about gaps in your notes and how they might be filled.

5 WHAT TO WRITE

Sometimes I learn the most when I am uncomfortable, unsure, and attempting new things. As you use new tools to observe and note events in your classroom, you may gain new learning and insights. But your first days and hours of taking notes may cause moments of discomfort and uncertainty. In fact, if your notes are to improve, chances are you have to seek out that discomfort by pushing yourself to reconsider what you write about.

This insight came to me the first time I took classroom notes that were completely random and unfocused. Previously, I had never tried to take notes without doing some mental sorting and censoring of myself. But on this day many years ago, I sat in a first-grade classroom, taking notes as a group of girls participated in writing workshop. In this class, students were allowed to talk about whatever they wanted to talk about during workshop time, to write about whatever they wanted to write about. Here are some of my notes:

Tammy is starting to write. She says, "I need a pink crayon. Sarah's got all the pink crayons." Sarah replies, "I do not. I brought my own crayons from home, see?" She pulls out a set of markers, throws a pink crayon at Tammy.

For ten minutes, all I did was write as fast as I could, detailing this insipid little scene of kids arguing over the crayons and who had a right to possess them. Most previous mornings, I would have quickly moved to another table. But on this morning, I was determined to follow the advice of my graduate school professor. He had admonished me that week to stay put in one spot and write as much as I could about whatever I saw, not censuring my writing.

When I looked over my notes that afternoon, I could actually feel my face getting red. "Tammy then grabbed a pink crayon from Lisa." These were the scribblings of a moron! There wasn't a shred of insight into the writing processes of these kids. Here I was, almost finished with a graduate degree in literacy, and this was the best I could muster in my notetaking?

But the more I looked at these notes, the more I realized the kids spent *a lot* of time arguing over material goods in the writer's workshop. This led me eventually to see some of the underlying tensions in the workshop between the egalitarian values of the teacher and the more materialistic values of the kids. Some of my most original research began the day I stopped censuring my notes and really concentrated on just writing down what I saw.

You have to give yourself permission to write freely. Words, phrases, random and seemingly trivial details need to land on the page when you are learning to take notes. These notes shouldn't have a polished feel to them. They will lack insight. I think teachers do a whole lot of editing of what they are seeing and writing when they take notes because they don't want to be in the position I was, seeing what I had written as simplistic, rough, uninsightful. But that is exactly what you're going to need if you want to get fresh perspectives on some of the intractable issues in your classroom.

Too often, we write our observations within a firmly established context of what we think our classroom *is*. We want to believe we've created a democratic place, where reading and writing are valued, where students treat each other fairly. This may be true much of the time. But the times when it is not true are the times when both teachers and students are ripe for learning. Raw notes—just writing what you see, as fast as you can, without editorial comment or deletions—can get you to that clear picture of what your classroom is.

These raw notes are the raw materials from which your research or assessments can grow. They will contain gems, nuggets of truth that will shape the rest of your notetaking agenda. But these nuggets will have to be mined in the future.

The notes you take quickly each day won't be the whole narrative, the complete story. And they shouldn't have the smooth feel of telling the whole story of any child or day in the classroom. But they will have the ingredients you need to tell the story of one student, one class, or one curricular idea.

Taking raw notes is the process of gathering raw ingredients. You will need time later to measure, weigh, mix, and cook what you've gathered into some kind of final product. But remember that this does come *later*. You're on a shopping expedition now, getting the freshest, most useful materials out of your classroom.

As you begin to take notes, keep the following principles in mind. They will help you continue your observations when you're feeling unconfident about your skills.

Write the Unwritable

Most teachers seem to follow that Midwestern principle of better living in their notetaking—if you can't say something nice, don't say anything at all. But the most interesting and useful information in your classroom may make you blush. Give yourself permission to write the most inconsequential garbage in the world. You're trying to see students in new ways, and that requires really being open to what you're seeing around you. If you get stuck, consider these questions: What surprises you? Bothers you? Worries you? Write down observations that would make you cringe if others read them—Melissa whacking John on the arm during the science experiment (is it anger or first love?); the whole class discussion of *Charlotte's Web* that shows only half the class read the assigned chapters; the planned lesson on quotation marks that blossoms into an unexpected and animated discussion of idioms. If you get stuck, give yourself some prompts to keep going. Write "I see," "I hear," or "I wonder" and fill in your own blanks.

Just Count

If words get in the way for you, begin your notetaking by keeping tally sheets. Many teachers have had terrible experiences as writers, and it's not surprising that they struggle to write anything when it's time to take notes. If you are one of these teachers, you may want to ease into notetaking by keeping tally sheets. To tally, you begin with a list of students you are observing in their whole class or small group. You check off who talks and how often each student contributes to the group.

Marilyn Chesley wanted to look at the kinds of talk in her small fourth-grade literature groups and to know who talked the most. Her tally sheet began with a notation for who spoke how often and gradually changed to considering the kinds of responses in the literature group (see Figure 5.1).

Gail Bussiere was concerned that she might be treating students differently in her reading groups. So she tallied the number of semantic or phonetic cues she gave to different readers in groups, and then she compared totals in these different groups (see Figure 5.2 on page 40).

Joni Cooke was looking at gender differences in her literature discussion groups. She looked at same-sex groups discussing different books and noted not only how much students talked, but also what the differences were in her response pattern when she worked with all-boy or all-girl groups (see Figure 5.3 on page 41).

FIGURE 5.1   Marilyn's Discussion Group Tally

Discussion Group

Discussion Group	Teacher	Karen	Susan	Beth	Joe	Tim	Totals
Elaboration	4	0	8	5	4	2	23
Feedback	15	0	4	1	1	0	21
Topic Change	0	0	0	0	0	0	0
Interruptions	0	0	1	0	0	0	1
Directions	2	0	0	0	0	0	2
Procedure	0	9	5	9	7	8	38
Questions	24	3	8	5	3	3	46
Reading	0	1	1	1	1	1	5

Discussion Group	Teacher	Karen	Susan	Beth	Joe	Tim	Totals
# of Turns	43	13	26	21	17	13	133
# of Words	464	94	198	360	242	132	1490
Average Words per Turn	10.8	7.2	7.6	17.1	14.2	10.2	11.2

Discussion Group	Teacher	Students	Girls	Boys
# of Turns	43	90	60	30
# of Words	464	1026	652	374
Average Words per Turn	10.8	11.4	10.9	12.5
% of Turns	32.3	67.7	45.1	22.6
% of Words	31.1	68.9	43.8	25.1
# of Words Read	0	303	176	127
% of Words Read	0	100	58.1	42

Discussion Group	Girls	Boys
# of Turns Each	20	15
# of Words Ea.	217	187
% of Turns Ea.	15	11.3
% of Words Ea.	14.6	12.6

FIGURE 5.2   Gail's Reading Clues Checklist

Reading Clues Checklist		
Teacher **Mrs. Bussiere** Date		
GROUP & BOOK	PHONETIC	SEMANTIC
#2 Geraldine's Big Snow (continuation)	//// ④	HHT HHT // ⑫
#3 Let's Tell Time	⓪	HHT HHT / ⑪
#1 The Snow	//// ④	HHT ⑤
#1 Ten Bears in My Bed	//// ④	HHT HHT / ⑪
#2 Little Bear's Friend Chapter 2	// ②	HHT ⑤

Tina Meserve wanted to see how different instructional contexts affected the responses of her students. So she tallied the number of responses by students during three different periods: a student-directed problem-solving period; a music class led by another teacher; and a child-abuse presentation by an advocacy group (see Figure 5.4 on page 42).

Heidi Stanhope was concerned about the participation of her special needs students in small group activities, so she sat in as an observer on two different groups that mixed her special needs students with

FIGURE 5.3 Joni's Tally of Gender Differences in Literature Discussion Groups

Students and Teacher Response		
Student Names	Responses	*Lost on a Mountain in Maine*
Josh	45	
Ken	16	
Justin	32	
Edward	39	
Matt	46	
Total Student	178	
Teacher	40	
Total Number & T.	218	
Students Names	Responses	*Sarah, Plain and Tall*
Abby	23	
Betsy	42	
Sarah	7	
Total Student	72	
Teacher	58	
Total Number & T.	130	

other class members, and noted how many responses came from each student (see Figure 5.5 on page 43).

Many teachers find that tallying oral responses is the best way into notetaking. One teacher wrote after completing a tally sheet, "This gives me just enough information to know where to begin. I hardly knew what to look for when I started this project. Now I have some idea of what to look at and write about."

Work to Eliminate Prefab Judgments in Your Notes

By "prefab" judgments, I mean those insights in your notes that are based not upon what you're seeing but upon your preconceptions of what your classroom is like and how learning occurs in it.

FIGURE 5.4

Tina's Tally of Different Instructional Contexts (✔ indicates response by student; ⟨✔⟩ indicates response initiated by teacher [for music class only])

	Student Directed Problem-Solving Discussion	Music Class Teacher Directed Lesson	Child Abuse Presentation from Child Advocacy Group
Carrie	✔✔✔✔	⟨✔⟩⟨✔⟩	
Kate	✔✔✔✔✔✔		✔
Amy	✔✔✔✔	⟨✔⟩	✔
Philippa	✔✔✔✔		✔✔✔
Mandy	✔✔		
Jennifer	✔✔✔	✔	✔
Kimberly	✔✔		
Ashley	✔✔✔		✔✔
Carol	✔✔	⟨✔⟩⟨✔⟩	
Nicole		✔✔✔	✔✔
Bob	✔✔✔		✔
Richard	✔✔✔✔✔	✔✔	✔✔✔✔✔
Tommy	✔✔✔✔✔✔✔	✔✔✔✔✔	✔✔
Scott	✔✔✔✔✔✔✔✔✔	✔	✔✔✔✔
Mike	✔✔✔	✔✔	✔
Kyle	✔✔✔✔✔✔✔✔	✔✔✔✔✔✔✔✔	✔✔✔✔✔
Tim	✔✔✔✔✔	✔✔	
Teddy			

Prefabricated homes come with all the design, materials, and construction predetermined. In many respects, they are as comfortable a home as those of an original design. But nothing about them is original—all the design and thinking has been done for the potential owner before the purchase.

Many times words and phrases show up in rough notes that demonstrate our own prefab thinking about students. We use words, phrases, and ideas we are comfortable with, but they can be a leap to a conclusion about our students and teaching that isn't warranted.

FIGURE 5.5 Heidi's Tally of the Participation of Her Special Needs Students

Reading Group

Reading Group	Teacher	Matt	Josh	Aaron	Kim	Nicole	Totals
Elaboration	6	1	1	0	1	0	9
Feedback	37	0	1	0	0	0	38
Topic Change	0	0	1	0	0	0	1
Interruptions	0	6	4	0	2	0	12
Directions	21	0	0	0	0	0	21
Procedure	0	2	3	0	1	0	6
Questions	15	0	0	1	0	1	17
Reading	0	9	10	6	5	6	36

Reading Group	Teacher	Matt	Josh	Aaron	Kim	Nicole	Totals
# of Turns	70	20	18	7	9	6	130
# of Words	412	95	78	43	52	39	719
Average Words per Turn	5.9	4.8	4.3	6.1	5.8	6.5	5.5

Reading Group	Teacher	Students	Girls	Boys
# of Turns	70	60	15	45
# of Words	412	307	91	216
Average Words per Turn	5.9	5.1	6.1	4.8
% of Turns	53.9	46.2	11.6	34.6
% of Words	57.3	42.7	12.7	30
Words Chorally Read		206		
Words Read Individually		206		

Reading Group	Girls	Boys
# of Turns Each	7.5	15
# of Words Ea.	45.5	72
% of Turns Ea.	5.8	11.5
% of Words Ea.	6.3	10

For example, you might write, "John seems to take risks and trusts his answers during the reading discussion." "Taking risks" and "trust" may reflect attributes that are valued in your classroom, but what exactly does this notation mean? It's better to write down what you saw and heard that day during the reading discussion—"John spoke out for the first time this year in reading group, saying, 'Carrie took my idea.'" Later, a pattern may emerge in your notes and observations that shows John fits *your* definition of a risk taker. But that jargon needs a clear definition, and you need to allow patterns to develop in your notes and observations over time before that judgment can be made.

As you start to take notes, the following activities can help you figure out what to write.

1. Practice with videotape segments.

Bring a videotape of your students at work to a meeting with a colleague or group, and then practice taking notes together. Compare what different group members write. What are the differences in your notes? In your perceptions? These discussions can help you develop a focus for improving your notes. For example, your colleague might include lots of quotes in the actual dialect of the students. In contrast, your strength might be a rich description of the social environment. Your colleague might note that one student is especially disruptive. You might see the same interactions differently—as a positive step for a student who has been inhibited in groups before. Talk about the differences in your notes, the influences that create those differences, and specific strategies you might develop for improving your notes.

2. Spend a week just counting.

Zero in on one issue that is important to you as a teacher, and see if you can find a way to tally responses, rather than write descriptions of what's going on. All you need to get started is a class list and an issue of interest. Some things you can count include:

▾ the number of turns taken by children;

▾ the frequency of change in the topic of conversation;

- the number of different students who change the conversation topic;

- the number of boys' versus girls' utterances;

- the number of responses in science workshop versus responses in writer's workshop;

- the ratio of your talk to children's talk;

- the number of new drafts of writing each child starts in one week.

Once you have a week or two of tallies, think about what you've learned from the tallies and how you might revise your notetaking to reflect this new knowledge.

3. Revise your notetaking forms.

If you know what the focus of your research or assessment will be, it makes sense to revise your record keeping forms to include a place for notes on this issue. Look at the forms you use now and see if there is a way to revise them to include space to write about "reading strategies" or "gender issues" or "social interactions." This will help remind you what you need to write about each day and keep you focused on your research and assessment topics.

6 WHAT TO DO WITH WHAT YOU'VE WRITTEN

O nce you get into the habit of taking notes daily, you'll also want to get in the habit of "cooking" your notes. "Cooking" involves some sort of daily analysis of what you've written. You can cook your notes in the midst or after the fact, but it's important that you continually put what you've written into the larger context of your research or assessment questions.

Historically, the models for cooking notes and observations have come from anthropological studies. While looking at what anthropologists do can provide some insight for teachers, I think in many ways these models are inappropriate. They contribute to that "superteacher" syndrome I mentioned early in the book and make teachers feel very insecure and inadequate in their notetaking.

Let's be realistic. A typical anthropologist who has been airlifted into the bush in deepest Africa or Bora Bora spends all day with the tribe. That is her whole life. She takes notes. At night, in her hut by the light of a candle, she laboriously "cooks" her notes till she has reams of detailed observations and analyses.

That anthropologist will be an appropriate role model for my life as a researcher only if she's got a husband in the hut, desperate to find his maroon socks before his big meeting in the morning, and a daughter who nonchalantly announces her final science report on acorns (which she hasn't started writing yet) is due the next day. Add a television blaring in the corner, and if this researcher still manages to cook up forty pages of notes each night then I'll be impressed.

The lives of most anthropologists or even full-time educational researchers who are held up as models for teachers are not even remotely similar to the professional existence of most teachers who daily take notes and seek to analyze them. The suggestions in this chapter acknowledge that our time is short and the needs of our students are great. But within those constraints, you can still systematically begin to analyze and improve what you've written in your notes. The following strategies for cooking notes are easy to attempt and will likely bring marked improvement to your notes in a short period of time.

Add Quotes to Your Notes

If you're not sure what to write, write down exactly what you are hearing from students. The more you include the real words of your students, the more you will be able to move away from your biases into a more accurate representation of what's going on in your classroom.

One of the flaws in many assessment narratives and research reports from teachers is the quality of the quotes from students. Too often, what's captured is the idea of the child unconsciously transcribed into the dialect of the teacher. If you write down just what you hear, in the student's own words, you will have a terrific record down the road of your student's development. The culture of your classroom is revealed by the language in it, and you'll want to have a record of that.

Depending upon the purpose of your notes, you may want to tape-record class interactions for transcription later and note nonverbal behaviors during your notetaking in the classroom. Penny Nutting was studying whole group discussions in her classroom. Penny ran a tape recorder to capture student interactions orally, without noting these interactions during class time. Instead, she wrote down students' non-verbal behaviors during this discussion. She looked for patterns within these interactions and chose to transcribe only small segments of talk to highlight the patterns she was seeing during these discussions. Her final transcript includes both the words of the students, in the left-hand column, and her more global analysis, or "cooking," of what was going on, in the right-hand column (see Figure 6.1).

QUESTION YOURSELF AND ADD QUESTIONS TO YOUR NOTES

These questions might be to yourself or, if you're a brave soul, to anyone else (students or colleagues) who will look at the notes. Questions to consider adding to your notes at various points include:

- Why did I think this was important to write down?

- How does this connect with what I saw earlier in the day, week, year?

- Based upon what I'm seeing, what action should I take to change the curriculum?

These questions will help you figure out what the purposes of these rough notes might be. Do they fit in with a research question you have? With a curricular change you are considering? With an assessment narrative you're planning to write for a particular child?

These questions can easily be abbreviated in your notes. For example, thinking about the importance of what you're noting becomes *I?* Issues of curricular change become *C?* Potential additions to assessment narratives become *A?* What you're trying to do is develop a

FIGURE 6.1   Penny's Final Transcript

Dinosaurs Before Dark
A Single-Book Group Discussion

Teacher: How do you know that?

Abby: ...I don't know. I just guessed. Ah, Dinosaurs were made before people.

Teacher: Dinosaurs were made before people. Anybody else have an idea? Or a thought about that?

Beth: I think they were. Cavemen. When the dinosaurs were. 'Cause I read a book about it. Cavemen used to hit 'em with their clubs.

Tom [interrupting]: They used a club?? To hit dinosaurs??

John: Dinosaurs and men were never there at the same time.

Tom: They DID TOO. Only cavemen, but not real people like us right now. Only CAVEMEN.

Richard: I don't believe this.

Tom: I do too.

Teacher: Why don't you believe it Richard? [He giggles]

Richard: Oh boy. I don't even think there's such a thing as cavemen. 'Cuz if there was, I'm thinking they would live inside the moon.

Tom: Is your cousin the man on the moon or something, Richard?
<u>Yah but almost ALL the books about dinosaurs say stuff about cavemen at the same time of dinosaurs.</u>

Richard: Yah because probably they, if they were hungry, they would just slice their legs off and eat them...What are you doing, Tom?

Tom: Trying not looking. 'Cuz I don't believe you.

I was hoping someone would have convincing evidence about cavemen vs. the dinosaur. Abby, in typical female fashion, did not assert herself.

John has no proof for Tom.

And Richard is also not convincing. Instead, he becomes silly.

Tom is quick with a comeback and uses a very sarcastic tone of voice.

Tom does not find what Richard is saying to be funny. At this point, the conversation disintegrates and I realize that I'm not going to get a correct answer from the students. I figure others in the class must also be dealing with the same misinformation and I will make sure that we watch the video Myth vs. Reality, a show that talks about the existence of dinosaurs.

mindset that constantly questions as you write your notes, that maximizes the value of the time you spend writing notes by trying to fit the pieces you're gathering from your classroom into larger puzzles.

VARY YOUR NOTES

Even though I've emphasized consistency throughout this handbook, there are times when you'll want to be inconsistent as a way to get out of notetaking ruts. For example, it's only natural that some students will show up in your notes much more than others. After you've been taking notes for a while, you'll want to scan them quickly to see who rarely shows up in your observations. No teacher manages to observe all children equally—we have cultural biases and personal preferences that cause all of us to focus on some students more than others. After you determine what small handful of students rarely appear in your notes, make an effort to spend a day of notetaking time only writing about those students. This can be a powerful tool for improving your teaching, as William Ayers (1993) writes:

> The goal of observation is understanding, not some imagined objectivity. If a teacher is invested in and fascinated by a child—if the child is a "favorite"—that is not a problem. The teacher will always be working to understand and teach that child. The problem is when the child is unseen, invisible, or not cared for—and this is not a problem of objectivity but of commitment. Pushing oneself to see and observe and understand this child—and every child—is an act of compassion and an important part of teaching. (37)

Some of the most interesting discussions I've had with colleagues have been around notes focused on those students we neglect in our observations. It's a terrific way to tease out your values as a teacher and to renew your commitment to all students in your care.

In the same way, if you tend to write only quotes of students, spend a week of notetaking where you note only nonverbal behaviors. Or if you never write quotes, do the reverse—write only quotes. Within the boundaries of consistent daily notetaking, varying what you write can make the task new again when you're beginning to feel yourself in a rut of observing and writing the same kinds of notations daily.

CODE YOUR NOTES

Codes can help you sort, analyze, and limit the ways you use your notes. And there is going to be a point where you will want some limits or boundaries in order to get a clear sense of how notetaking can work for you.

Early in any notetaking project, I find it helpful to use the Levi-Strauss codes, adapted by Corsaro (1981): *MN* for methodological notes and *TN* for theoretical notes. Methodological notes include questions or statements about *how* you're doing your work. They might be statements like "I should put a tape recorder by the science center to get those interactions" or "Maybe students should keep logs of questions asked during literature discussions" or "I'm getting interrupted all the time! Maybe I need a mini-lesson on how to get help during writer's workshop without bothering the teacher!"

Theoretical notes include any hunches about patterns or *why* events are occurring as they are. A theoretical note might be as formal as "I think Tadd's behavior supports Graves' theory about the revision process in writing." But most are less formal—they are those "aha" moments that are essential to good teaching. These might include statements like "I think Jennifer is responding more during whole class discussions because I've required small group exchanges—maybe that's building her confidence?" or "Perhaps Jason's frustration in science is due to so many absences in the past two weeks—the group seems unwilling to bring him up to date on the project."

You can also code your observations according to curricular area or social interactions among students. During a summer literacy enrichment program, one team of teachers used the following codes to denote when notes on individual children in the program were written: *R* (for reading time), *C* (for free choice time), *S* (for spelling time), and *W* (for writing time). They combined these with other letters that detailed whom the child worked with—*T* (for teacher), *A* (for alone), and *S* (for other students). Observations of each student were coded so that any teacher on the team analyzing them would have a social and curricular context for the notations (see Figure 6.2).

REARRANGE YOUR NOTES

Just changing the way the page is set up to take notes can make a big difference in what you write and can ensure you get the information you need. Teachers working together in the same enrichment program were trying to focus on strategies children use in developing reading skills. They revised their notetaking form to include a space for reading strategies; this simple change made notes on strategies a priority (see Figure 6.3).

In another situation, a team of teachers was considering Eric's behavior during reading and writing time. They all took notes individually on address labels. When it came time to consider the patterns of his literacy behavior and his development as a reader and writer, they arranged all the labels on one side of a series of pages. This provided room for collective notes and insights about what these random observations said about Eric's development (see Figure 6.4).

There aren't any easy prescriptions for how you should cook your notes—so much depends upon what your notes are for and who you are as a teacher and learner. But the following activities can give you a better sense of yourself as an observer and help you analyze, revise, and improve your notes on a daily basis.

1. Develop some codes for your notes.
Remember to keep it simple—if you have more than three or four codes, it will be hard for you to keep up with them. You might start

FIGURE 6.2   Coded Observations on Labels

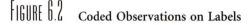

Anecdotal Notes

7-5 Ethan negative about day.
"That doesn't look like a web."
Warmed up as morning progressed.
Asked frequently "What do I do now?"

Ethan   (WT) ——————————— Writing with Teacher
   Walked around the room for
~ 2-3 min. trying to find an idea,
but quickly came to one   7/6

Ethan   Watching/looking (RA) ——————————— Reading Alone
        Looking at tapes in basket.
RT Bean bag - Little attention to base
7/6 ball book - Read over Zach's shoulder
     Disc Book together

Ethan - (RT) con't - Block top
over face - yawning - Became
involved when we read as a sm.
gp. Chose poems to be read Aloud.
7/6 Makes comments & facial Expressions negative

Choice ——————— 7/6 CT Ethan chose frog center
with   but left it and decided to
Teacher   draw with Alan

Ethan - ST - 7/7
Very attentive - sat back by
picnic table. made several
   comments.

                                     Ethan
Morning mess - Read very loudly
& clear beg. got softer & less (RA)
involved as message went on.
"I know whats gonna happen because
my teacher told me & I read it ... See "

W.T.
Ethan sat next to Andrew and
copied the info. that Andrew's
dad had written about WWII.

FIGURE 6.3   Reading Workshop Conference Log

Reading Workshop   Student Name   Paula
Conference Log

Book- Cookies, Snakes, Birthday Cake

Date- 7-11   Teacher-   Kelly

Retelling for Cookies
      -Very surfaced retelling, retold the pictures but was able
to add some personal information. Was able to tell a lot about
the pictures b/c of a strong vocabulary   bee = honey
      cow = milk

Strategies - started on the right page
          - Stayed with story pattern and finished the pattern by
using picture clues
          - when one word was on a page she would use beginning
sounds when coaxed   "s-s-s. shake."

Observations -knew where the words were on the page and ran
      her finger under them when "reading" the words

Book- The Birthday Cake "

Date- 7/12   Teacher- Karen

Retelling

Strategies Pictures
Knew beginning letters & sounds of color words

Observations Paula came up to me "I can read this
book." When she started she made a sentence close to
the one in the book so I showed her how part of
what she said was really in the book. Then she attended
well to the words & looked & verbalized the beginnings of
them.

FIGURE 6.4   **Labels with Notes on Eric's Development**

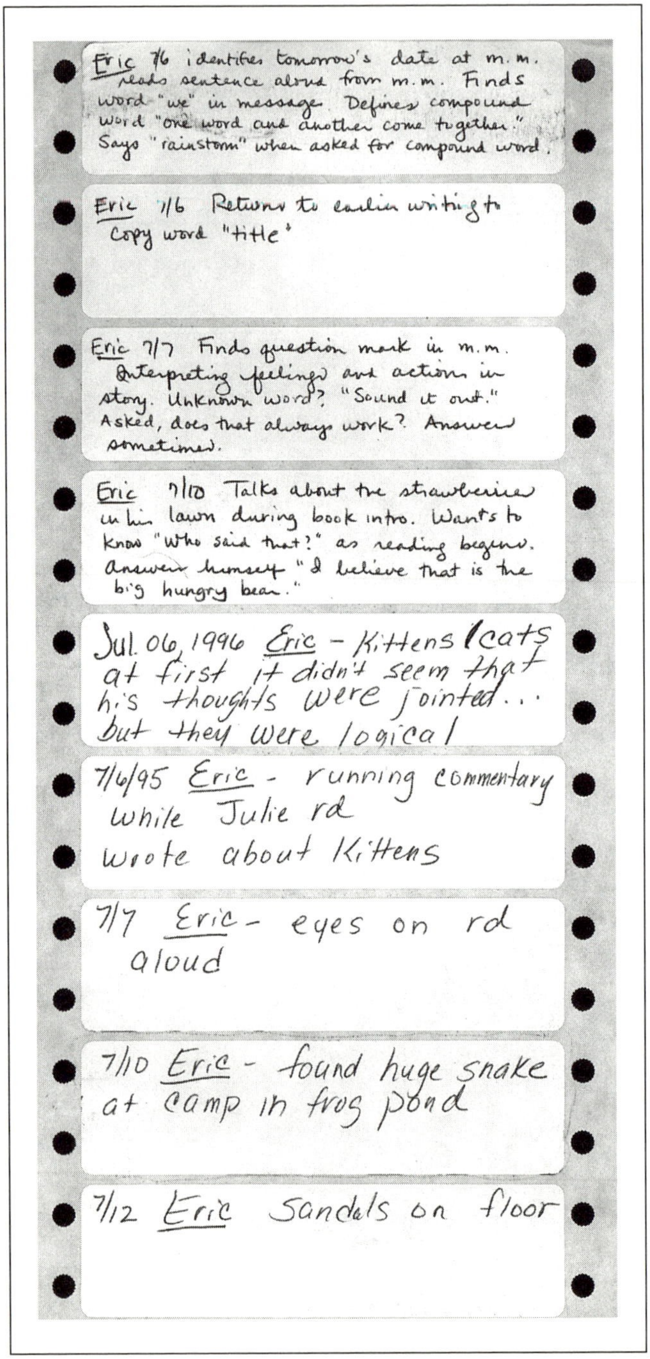

Eric 7/6 identifies tomorrow's date at m.m. reads sentence aloud from m.m. Finds word "we" in message. Defines compound word "one word and another come together." Says "rainstorm" when asked for compound word.

Eric 7/6 Returns to earlier writing to copy word "title"

Eric 7/7 Finds question mark in m.m. Interpreting feelings and actions in story. Unknown word? "Sound it out." Asked, does that always work? Answers sometimes.

Eric 7/10 Talks about the strawberries in his lawn during book intro. Wants to know "Who said that?" as reading begins. Answers himself "I believe that is the big hungry bear."

Jul. 06, 1996 Eric - Kittens/cats at first it didn't seem that his thoughts were jointed... but they were logical

7/6/95 Eric - running commentary while Julie rd wrote about kittens

7/7 Eric - eyes on rd aloud

7/10 Eric - found huge snake at camp in frog pond

7/12 Eric Sandals on floor

with methodological or theoretical note codes. Or you may choose to pick two or three themes that are emerging in your notes and develop a simple scheme for coding these elements. If you find yourself getting confused, or if the coding is too time-consuming, abandon it. You can always develop codes or look for patterns later, after you have collected many different notes from observing your students.

2. Find and analyze judgmental statements in your notes.

Take a week's worth of notes and underline any words that could be seen as prefab judgments. Look closely, not only at verbs like *risks* and *trusts* and *honors,* but also at adjectives like *disruptive.* Examine those words that naturally provoke an emotional response in readers. Think back—can you remember the specific behavior or behaviors that sparked the judgments or emotions these words evoke? Set a goal of eliminating some of these words from your notes and consciously noting behaviors instead.

3. Underline jargon du jour in your notes.

There is a garden of words out there, and in every profession some words blossom and bloom for awhile, until they are so overused they lose their beauty and become like the dead lilies on your table that should have been discarded a week ago. Look for these words in your notes. For a while in the 1980s the word *process* was so prevalent in everything I wrote that I had to make a conscious effort to avoid using it. *Share* occupied the same prominent position in the early 1990s. Now I'm looking closely at every use of *fresh* and *sparks* in my writing. If you attend to your own jargon when you're taking notes, you'll be a better writer, especially when it comes to putting your notes into narrative form.

4. Take notes on the "unseen students" for one week.

After you identify the few students who rarely appear in your notes, choose one or two of these students and note their behaviors for a week. You will be amazed at what you learn about these "invisible" students—and about your own prejudices as a notetaker.

7 BRINGING IT ALL TOGETHER: TWO TEACHERS

By now if you've followed the advice in this handbook, your hands may be smudged with a bit of blue from the carbons of notes you've kept. You may be starting to get a sense of how to cook those notes, observing and assessing after the fact. You may know some of your colleagues and their students better after completing the activities from these pages with them. You have bits and pieces of new knowledge about how you might observe your students and note their growth as learners in new ways.

But your teaching life still rushes at you. There are materials to be photocopied for tomorrow's science workshop, phone calls to be made to reserve the bus and scare up chaperones for next week's field trip, and a curriculum meeting tomorrow to look at how your literacy program fits with the new state-mandated standards. The big question remains: How can what you want to do with notes, observations, and assessment fit in with what you *need* to do as a teacher?

The answer can't be found in any exhortations or bromides from me. It is found in the lives of individual teachers attempting to apply principles of thoughtful inquiry to their teaching, in the midst of all the constraints public schools impose that work to impede their effort.

I present two very real teachers to you, third-grade teacher Jennifer Allen of Gardiner, Maine, and high school English teacher Kim Campbell of Portland, Oregon. These are teachers who observe students regularly, take notes, and use these notes to complete teacher research in the classrooms, to write assessments, and to change their curriculum. They long ago abandoned any ideal concept of what they might be as observers and inquirers, and instead use notetaking strategies that fit the needs and quirks of their lives and those of their students.

The teachers are in very different instructional settings. Jennifer usually works with 20 students in a rural elementary school. Kim has taught up to 160 students at a time in a large Oregon high school but is in the midst of a change to a new role as a teaching principal at an urban high school. Obviously, the differences between working with 160 students and with 20 students cause differences in the ways that the teachers observe students, take notes, and use these observations. But I suspect you'll also be surprised at the many similarities between these teachers who work at opposite ends of the country, with very different students. Perhaps the greatest similarity between Jennifer and Kim is that their observation and notetaking systems are still evolving, and probably always will be.

Opening Everything to Question: Jennifer Allen

Jennifer Allen is twenty-six years old, just finishing a master's degree in education. She is completing her fifth year of teaching. She has written grants and served on district committees to change the report card and to implement portfolio assessment programs in local schools.

The focus of many of Jennifer's notes and observations is her literacy program. Learning to take notes in the midst of teaching was not an easy process for Jennifer. She explains, "It was hard for me to get into a rhythm. When I first began to take notes about my students during reading time, I didn't know what I was writing, and it just seemed to be a mess—very frustrating and murky."

Jennifer was able to continue to write notes, even when she wasn't sure of the usefulness of them, because she knew this was a habit she needed to develop as a teacher. "What I made a commitment to, and it's the commitment I've kept, is writing fifteen minutes a day. It's like brushing your teeth, or exercising. If you can get to the point where it's a habit, it isn't hard at all anymore. It's just getting to the point where it's a habit that is rough!"

Jennifer eventually found her notes served dual purposes—they became a key component of her assessment system, and they were a daily data source for the two-year teacher-research project she conducted in her classroom on the role of students in peer-led literature circles.

Assessing Students

Jennifer found the time to build an assessment program out of her observational notes by looking critically at all the other assessments she did of students and making some choices. She says, "I find many teachers do assessments on kids that aren't needed, especially at my level—third grade. They take techniques they've learned at a Reading Recovery workshop or a whole language conference and use them on all kids. It's enormously time-consuming to do miscue analyses and running records on every single child multiple times during the year, and it's not needed." Jennifer found in reading that she didn't need to use so many assessment tools with each student. "I do a running record or a miscue analysis at the start of the year—this gives me baseline information, and throughout the year these are assessments that can help with certain children. But with the ones who have cracked the code, I'm looking for different information. I really think with every assessment about whether this evaluation tool is going to give me useful information or not, and whether it's really worth the time or if it's going to bog me down."

What is consistent are the notes Jennifer takes every day in her classroom. That's the one tool that's flexible enough to allow her to look at different kids differently. Jennifer asks questions as she writes her notes during reading time. What strategies does this child use in reading? How do they work with others? What books engage them?

She explains her process: "I keep these notes on Post-its, and I write for fifteen minutes a day. Each Post-it has the child's name on top that I am observing. You really wouldn't understand many of these notes—they're in my own personal shorthand. It's a word or two that sparks a memory or an idea for me that ends up on the Post-it. But they are *for* me, for my assessments, so it doesn't matter at this stage whether or not they make sense to other people" (see Figure 7.1).

These notes are then filed for each child: "At some point in the day, I slap the Post-its into an old grading roster that was given to me when I started the job. It has each student's name tabbed in it, and that's where the Post-its for that child go. If you open up that notebook, it isn't pretty, and I'm the only one who could tell you what I mean on many of those Post-its, but over time I get lots of information on most children."

These notes are supplemented with assessments and interviews that do make sense for the student or the class as a whole, and they form the basis of Jennifer's assessment of students (see Figure 7.2).

Jennifer still has to fill out quarterly rank cards, but these aren't something she puts lots of energy into. It is the other assessments, built around her records and the actual work of the kids, that the parents and Jennifer really value. Even though Jennifer had a strong role in developing the report card, she sees its limitations. "We tried to include language about development and phases. I now see the report card shouldn't be an instructional tool—I want the parents of my students to understand the language we use. I want my assessment system to communicate to them their child's strengths and needs. It's hard to do that with any report card."

In the fall, Jennifer has a conference with the parents of each child individually: "I work from my notes to talk with them, but it's really just about my initial observations, concerns, and questions. At this point, my notes aren't organized in any fashion. I want my conferences to be relaxed, and I want to listen closely to the parents." Jennifer

FIGURE 7.1 Post-its Help with Assessment

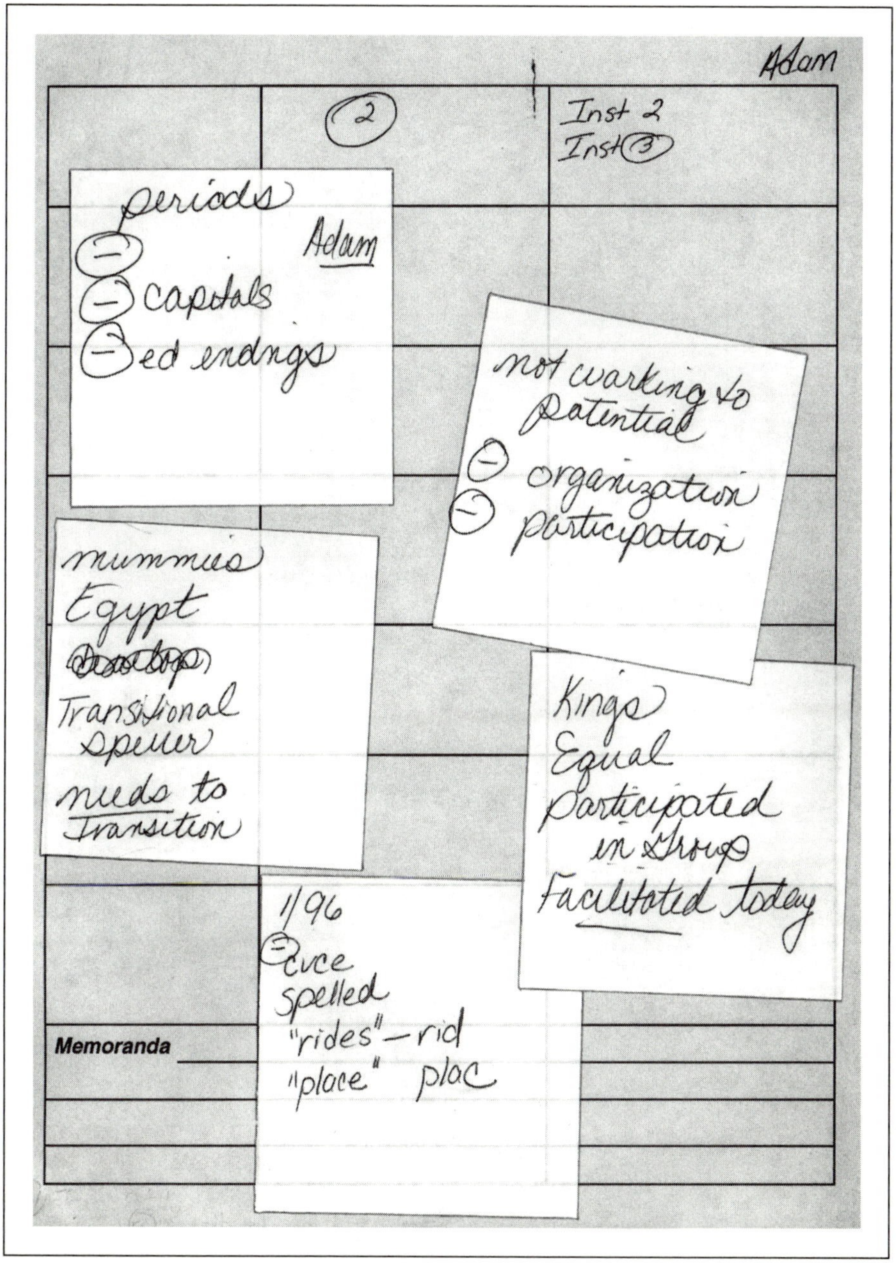

FIGURE 7.2   Jennifer's Whole Class Math Assessment Notes

Math ①   Quarter 1st

Names	probability	Addition Subtract Regrouping	Place Value	Comparing (Treating +3)	Problem Solving	Money	Time
John	–	– pictures + Symbol Some	Read + write thousands hundreds	+	–	+ add + variety coins	+ 1 hour 2-four minutes
Craig	+	+ with pictures	+ 10	+	x		minute
Amanda (base facts)	–	① works on subt. w/ pictures	thousands through hundred	work on reading	– reading tree diagram	+	⊕ hour ⊖ minute
Khalan (Base facts)	+	+ Symbols	+	+			+
Jillian	+	② Subtract sm picture ⊖ Big numbers work on	Hundreds work thousands				+
Jacob	+	+ Symbolism subtraction pictures	read to 1,000	+	organized lists logic exce llent	adds variety coins	+
Carrie	–	+ Symbolism	+	+	–	values adding on @ pennies	– minute
Dan	+	+ symbolism – Symbolism	+	+	organized lists	decimal	+
Ryan (Basic Facts)	+	+ symbolism + with picture	read number write 2,026	+	picture logic	+	+
Carol		+ Symbolism	understand thousands	+	confidence	+	+ hours
Riley (counts 5)	+	– pictures ① working on ⊖ writes	understand through thousands ⊖ writes	⊖ reading ⊖ reading numbers	+	+ adds. variety coins ID value	+
Pete	–	① more pictures Symbolism picture life	through 1,000	+	takes risks	+	⊖ minute
Donna	–	⊖ Symbol		work on			– ½ hr

believes if she spent lots of time organizing what she would say, it would take time away from listening closely to the parents.

The second quarter, at the end of January, is when Jennifer does a lengthy written narrative assessment of each child. "This is time-consuming, so I begin in December and complete the process by mid-January. This time of year, with the break, is a good reflective time for me." Jennifer wants to do some focused thinking about each child in an intensive way at this point in the year, so that she has sufficient time to meet the needs of students that will show up in these narratives by the end of the school year.

Since this is the narrative that will be placed in the child's cumulative folder, Jennifer takes the time to organize her notes and thoughts. She explains, "I make sure all the Post-its are in the book, and then I use an evaluative worksheet I've developed to see where the holes are for each child (see Figure 7.3). My notes are rough on these guide sheets, but I get a sense of whom I need to be observing more closely. I then take the time to observe those children more closely during the next few weeks before I finish the narratives."

In writing the narratives, Jennifer always begins with the students who are "easiest"—the ones she feels she knows best and can write about with authority (see Figure 7.4). The first narratives still take almost an hour each to craft. By the time she has completed the first third of her narratives, the process only takes thirty minutes per child. But by the time she reaches the last third, the writing for each child is back to an hour or more.

"Even though those final students are enigmatic, the process is smoother because I've worked out some of the kinks and gotten into a rhythm with the earlier narratives," says Jennifer. Many teachers make the mistake of trying to write the most difficult narratives first. They then become so discouraged by the process that they abandon it. When you begin with the children you know well, you're able to get into a rhythm and build some speed for writing something about more challenging students.

The main assessment in the third quarter is a student-led portfolio conference with parents. "I model this after Terri Austin's work (Austin 1994)," Jennifer explains. "By this time in the year, I want students to

FIGURE 7.3   Jennifer's Evaluation Worksheet on Lisa

NAME _Lisa_

READING   4

The King's Equal

variety of Biographys.

Piano Lessons can be murder – Gloce Pumps

appreciation for literature

— working on prefixes
= dictionary work
Character X punctuation.
for meaning
pauses at periods

WRITING   Persuasive Travel Brochure

+ capitals/periods   ✓ organization of thoughts

+ BME   ✓ punctuation accurately

✶ Conventional spelling   ✓ dev. voice/style

− add details

reach for Thesaurus → take risks with vocabulary

autobiography   revising independently

Come see
Real mummies
at the
Boston Museum

MATH

#-regrouping
multiplication
metric system
time

☐ ☐

Confidence.
risk taking

THEME   Mummies

ATTITUDE/EFFORT/QUALITY OF WORK

Responsible
Finisheson assignments

Becoming
more assertive (see Kristi)

FIGURE 7.4   Jennifer's Notes on Lisa

Lisa Smith

January 1996

Lisa is a responsible and conscientious student. She has developed strong study skills. Lisa writes down her homework assignments each day as she comes into class in the morning. She works hard to complete all assignments. Lisa is a quiet student who has a lot to offer in class discussions. She is continuing to become more assertive to get her ideas heard.

Lisa is at an instructional 4 reading level. She continues to develop solid reading habits and an appreciation for literature. Lisa has developed vocabulary strategies. She is becoming more successful at using the dictionary. She tries to figure out the word in context and then confirms her predictions using a dictionary. Lisa also breaks words down and infers meaning using her knowledge of prefixes (re, pre, dis). Lisa has a strong sense of story structure (beginning, middle, end). She has great insights into the characters and conflicts found within books. Lisa uses punctuation for meaning within stories. She is aware of the meaning of periods, quotation marks, and question marks. Lisa writes thoughtful responses to literature. Lisa is currently working on the book *The King's Equal*. Independently, she is reading books from the Goosebump collection. Lisa continues to develop strong inferential skills. This requires the students to look between and beyond the pages of the book.

In writing, Lisa recently created a travel brochure titled *Come See the Mummies at the Boston Museum*. She has demonstrated her understanding for persuasive writing. We are currently working on writing autobiographies. Lisa is working hard to write concise and detailed sentences. Lisa writes with a sense of beginning, middle, and end. We are working to organize information into paragraphs. This is a difficult skill and will take time to develop. We are continuing to work on using a variety of punctuation accurately within our writing. Lisa has transitioned to using mostly conventional spelling in her writing. Lisa has been introduced to the thesaurus. I am encouraging her to use this tool as a means to reach for richer vocabulary. We are also working on conferencing and revising our writing independently.

Lisa continues to take risks in math. She is developing a variety of problem-solving strategies and realizes that problem solving takes time and a lot of thinking. She has demonstrated her ability to solve problems involving logic. Lisa can solve addition and substraction problems that involve regrouping. We have also explored the metric system. She has demonstrated her understanding for centimeters, meters, and kilometers, and knows when a particular unit would be useful. We have also explored the concept of area and perimeter. She has a thorough understanding for the concept of multiplication. She understands what the numbers represent in multiplication sentences and can tell a story to convey its meaning. We are also looking at the concept of division and how it relates to multiplication.

Lisa is a sensitive person with a warm personality. She works well with her classmates. Lisa continues to develop confidence in the various subject areas. It's wonderful to see her smile when she is successful!

be taking responsibility for their learning. I also want them to be able to explain what they are learning to their parents. This assessment enables me to look at the children's growth as self-evaluators."

Surprisingly, the end of the year includes no major assessment outside of the required district rank cards. "I find at that point parents, kids, and teachers are often looking beyond this year to next year. Parents want to know what *next year's* teacher and requirements will be. I'm trying to tidy up lots of loose ends in the curriculum and to make sure we have a nice closure as a community to the year. I'm not going to write an assessment that just goes into a folder."

Jennifer's system makes me think about how much we do in schools that is driven by habit and not by careful thinking about the uses and purposes of observational records. Many districts that use a narrative assessment only use it at the end of the school year, when it is less likely to drive changes in curriculum. By using a range of assessments throughout the year, Jennifer is able to make changes "in the midst" that tie the curriculum closely to student needs.

Research

This function of using notes to change curriculum is nowhere more evident than in Jennifer's teacher research project considering the role of student facilitators in literature discussion groups. She explains, "My research question was pretty simple: What happens when student facilitators are used in literature groups?" She began with Harvey Daniels' (1994) guidelines for developing literature circles (see Figures 7.5a and 7.5b). Jennifer took regular notes, and she also completed student interviews and written inventories. Jennifer found that student notes and observations helped her develop a focus for the project. She explains, "I enlisted the students as co-researchers. At the end of each literature circle, I asked the facilitator to reflect on what went well for them, and what they would like to work on. These responses really helped me analyze the rest of my data" (see Figure 7.5c).

Jennifer found five "key words" or themes that showed up repeatedly in her data: *understanding* of text; *responsibility, respect* (self-

Figure 7.5A and B   Student Roles in Literature Circles (adapted from Daniels, 1994).

Student Roles in Literature Circles

REQUIRED ROLES	RESPONSIBILITY
Discussion Director	Thinks up discussion questions
Literary Luminary	Takes the group back to "memorable" sections of the text and reads them aloud to the group
Connector	Takes the readers from the text world to the real world
Illustrator	Creates a graphic response to literature

OPTIONAL ROLES

Researcher, Summarizer, Character Captain, Vocabulary Enricher, Travel Tracer

---

INVENTORY

NAME _____ AGE _____ DATE _____

What is the purpose for literature discussions?

Who is a good facilitator?

Why?

What makes a good discussion?

What does a facilitator do?

What does facilitate mean?

How did you learn to facilitate?

What would you like to do better as a facilitator?

FIGURE 7.5c   Reflection on Literature Discussion

Facilitator: _____Alex_____

Title of Book: _the family under the bridge_

Date: _4-1-96_

1. What went well about the discussion?

we built alot of one question

2. What did we learn new about the book that we didn't know before?

a lot of things you can hook into it

3. What do we want to work on?

We need to be a bit more serios

4. How do you feel as the facilitator today? Why?

I think I asked a good question because we built alot of it.

---

esteem), *listening*, and *participation*. She began to code her notes according to these themes that emerged, and her findings began to affect the ways the literature circles operated.

A new purpose of the circles evolved: to help students understand, analyze, and develop skills in group processes. "As a result of the students' feedback, I decided to incorporate the use of a tape recorder into our discussions. Students tape-recorded their discussions each day and processed it by listening to the tape. At the end of the discussion, students identified what went well and set new goals for the next day.

Students found that they needed to work on 'talking over' each other. They decided to pass the tape recorder among group members. They agreed that the one who spoke would hold the tape recorder," said Jennifer. She was amazed at the effectiveness of this strategy. Once students implemented this idea, the pace of the discussions slowed down dramatically, to the point where students were even responding to each other by name.

Jennifer has learned so much about her students by observing them, noting behaviors, asking students to do the same for each other, and then sifting through these observational records together. In writing up her research, she explained what it means to her. "When I think of what my research means to me, I'm reminded of a quote from Carl Rogers about purposes of learning: 'To free curiosity; to permit individuals to go charging off in new directions dictated by their own interests; to unleash the sense of inquiry; to open everything to questioning an exploration; to recognize that everything is in the process of change.' I certainly feel this way about myself. I'm always charging off in new directions with my research and assessment of students. But I'm more and more comfortable with this process of change."

JUGGLING, WONDERING, AND COLLABORATING: KIM CAMPBELL

Kim Campbell is a high school teacher who has recently been selected to serve as the teaching principal at a new high school in Portland, Oregon. Teaching is a second career for Kim. After working as a lawyer for a number of years, she returned to graduate school for her teaching certification. It is not uncommon for Kim to have five sections of students, with thirty students in each class. She is also married, with two preschool-aged children. Somehow she has to find a way to wear the hats of teacher, researcher, wife, and mom. She is honest in her assessment of this juggling act: "I won't lie and say I do it well most of the time. Often in the lunchroom I'm faced with the choice of eating my yogurt or writing my notes. I've learned to eat and write at the same time."

Kim has learned to adjust the ideals she reads about in textbooks to the realities of class after class of students charging in and out of her classroom. She explains, "With the numbers I deal with, I could never use my notes for assessments of individual students. But the notes are central for changing my curriculum and for keeping the students at the center of it."

Most of Kim's observational notes come from her teaching journal—a spiral-bound notebook with tear-out pages. She tries to write in it every day when the kids are in writing workshop or at the end of the day. She also keeps random notes when the class is doing an activity. "These are interspersed throughout the teaching journal, and you can see how spur-of-the-moment they are," she explains. "I've got sticky notes, scrap paper stapled in there. It may appear disjointed or disorganized, but it works for me."

Kim also keeps track of what the class has done each period, especially questions that come up in discussion, on a legal pad. "I photocopy these pages for the students who are absent in each class. It saves a lot of time to just hand someone who was absent these notes. They learn what was planned, but more importantly they see the questions that were generated by their classmates. Since my classes really run on these discussions, it puts the students who missed class right back into the thick of where we are."

For Kim, assessment, teaching, and research merge together readily through her notes. The notes help her make immediate changes in her teaching. "An example of how the notes change my plans can be found in this minilesson I did on my reading process," she explains. "In my first class, I brought in *Little House in the Big Woods* and talked about what that book meant to me as a child. I read the first chapter to that class. In my notes I wrote 'Boring! No one connects.' So later in the day, when I was doing that lesson with another class, I decided to read the pig-butchering chapter. In my notes I wrote 'Yeah!' They loved it! I also noted that Mary borrowed the book, and another student brought

FIGURE 7.6   Reading Workshop

Reading Workshop   9/14

Excerpt: <u>Little House in the Big Woods</u>
            Follow up to reading timeline
            + positive memories of being
            read to

    1st - opening chapter : BORING

    3rd - pig butchering - Yeah!
        Mary Sullivan borrows the book to
        read

    Share Groups:

    Current read/ Best or good reads

in *Green Eggs and Ham* later in the week, connecting with what I'd
talked about. It's those immediate changes that come from noting and
reflecting upon my students that make all the difference in the success
of what I do" (see Figure 7.6).

   Kim doesn't use her notes to write assessments of individual students. "With 150 students, it's impossible. For that assessment, the
notes from the students are helpful. They keep notes from their small
group discussions. I tend to keep track of who answered from each
group and track the kinds of questions generated. I will code these
with a series of slash marks, tallies, plusses, and minuses. Often I will
look at a pattern of questions generated in an early class and rethink
the questions I was planning to throw out at the start of a later group
of students."

   Kim takes notes when she walks around the room, often using

plusses and checks instead of words for much of what she is seeing. She says, "No one but me could possibly understand those notes. I fill in more words and phrases later in the day. But I understand the notes, and that's what matters" (see Figure 7.7).

Many times if the whole class is discussing a topic, Kim designates a notetaker to write the questions generated on the board. "My students always call the notetaker the 'Vanna White' person. It helps to have someone else responsible for that recording, so that I can stay involved in the conversation. Later I can jot down some of what's on the board after students leave."

Students are assessed using rubrics they develop with Kim. "When you have agreed-upon standards, it makes the individual assessments go smoothly. And I rely a lot on work samples—I'm famous for not returning work to students!" she explains.

The notes evolve into a research topic when something isn't working in Kim's class: "I find I need to start with something that's bothering me in my teaching in order to do research. That's the only way I'll stay highly motivated to carry through the research." One example of this research was a literature group project activity that was disastrous.

"I traced back through my notes, and I saw many instances where my enthusiasm and passion for the books I selected overrode looking closely at the students' responses," she explained. Kim had students write their honest responses to different parts of the curricular plan. She and the students compared these responses to the group discussion notes throughout the six weeks of the project. They developed a new assessment rubric together to replace the rubric Kim had devised on her own at the start of the project. Kim wrote up her findings from the research, and they were published (Campbell 1996).

"I would encourage anyone who is interested in notetaking and research to make sure you talk with students about what you're doing," said Kim. "It can be intimidating for students to see you walking around the room with a clipboard or notebook, writing. On the other hand, if you're honest with them, that this is a learning process for you and you're just trying to do a better job of understanding what your students need, they can be so helpful."

FIGURE 7.7   Editor's Draft

Editor's Draft handwritten notes:

10/24

Due: Editor's Draft

22/34 hand finished drafts — 1st period

1 had switched drafts

8 had no drafts

	1st	editor
Shelly	+	+	Beth ✓+ ✓+
Matt C.	✓++	✓+	
Ryan	+	+	No drafts
Kelli	+	+	Suzanne
Susan	+	+	Aaron
Wendy	✓+	+	Martin
Cara	+	✓++	
Molly	✓++	+	Rob
Nancy	+		Josh
Matt P.	+	✓++	Fran
Angela	✓+	+	
Jeremy	✓	✓	
James	✓	✓+	
Casey	✓++	+	
Vanessa	✓++	excused	
Heath	+	+	
Christine	✓	+	
John	+	+	
Lisa	+		
Becky	✓	✓++	
Joe	✓++	✓++	

late ed draft

(circled group:)
+ 27-30
      25
✓++ 24
✓+
✓   21

+ 14-15
✓++ 13
✓+ 11
✓ 10

Principles from Kim and Jennifer

Even though Kim and Jennifer work in different settings, with vastly different students, there are a few common principles they use for observing and assessing students. You might want to consider these as you look at the notes you make of students:

1. The notes are for the teacher.

When Kim and Jennifer share their notes on individual students, what they see may be just a word, a phrase, or just a check mark. These observations are for the teacher, so they don't try to meet some external standard of neatness, completeness, or depth of insight. Jennifer and Kim are concerned only that they can understand and use them to work with students. Many of us are locked into the "clean underwear" syndrome—we write out notes that are far more developed than they need to be. We have a fantasy or fear that someone will read these notes and not be able to make sense of them, thus thinking less of us as professionals. Both Kim and Jennifer use their notes to write assessments and research in a form that anyone could understand. But that comes late in the process. It isn't a part of their everyday notetaking.

2. Students are co-inquirers.

Jennifer and Kim depend upon their students for notes and observations. Both of their classrooms involve regular assignments for individual students to be recorders of small group and whole class comments and questions. It isn't an "extra" component of their notetaking—it's an essential aspect of being part of their classroom communities.

3. Continual assessment of what is working—and what isn't.

The notetaking is built from trying always to improve the learning environment in the classroom. As Kim explains, you'll stay more motivated if you use your notes to explore what *isn't* working with your students—these are the aspects of teaching and learning that are likely to hold your attention, and the notes should reflect that.

4. Focus on one issue and bring it to closure.
This is especially important if you plan to build a research agenda from your notes. It's interesting that Jennifer and Kim shared the same research question: What happens when students have certain responsibilities in literature discussion groups? It isn't surprising that this question held their attention, because literature circles are an exciting but often murky mix of responses to books and the sharing of lives. The rules for how these groups can work well are emerging and are going to vary from community to community. Closure for both Jennifer and Kim involved writing up their work in a way that summarized what they learned, and presenting this writing to a larger community.

8 FROM STEP-BY-STEP TO A DANCE: BUILDING A COMMUNITY OF NOTETAKERS

One of the most important discoveries we've made about children's development in the past few decades is that it's not a linear process. Beyond height and shoe size, almost no growth up or out occurs without some regression down or in. Students in classrooms make a few steps or even a leap forward in their understanding of literacy principles or a scientific concept, only to regress a few days or weeks later. And social interactions with other children, no matter how complex and chaotic, are essential for their continued development.

The same developmental principles apply to your growth as an observer and notetaker. If you try out the ideas and activities in this handbook, you will progress. But for most readers, every four steps forward will involve at least two steps backward. It is a slow process of improvement, because what you're trying to develop are new habits in your classroom. Be kind to yourself. Remember that your old habits as a teacher and learner took years to develop. You need to allow yourself time to develop new habits as an observer and notetaker, and not get discouraged at the natural regressions that will be part of the process.

I've tried in this handbook to take you step-by-step through activities and principles that can help you develop observation and notetaking skills. But maybe the linear nature of the book is dishonest. We all know no one develops step-by-step as a teacher—it's really more of a dance, and it's always about learning some new steps along the way. I want to close out the handbook with some suggestions for ways to keep moving forward in your development. Dances usually work best if more than one person is involved. Most teachers who develop the habit of keeping observational notes have one thing in common, no matter what their school setting. They have people who support their work. It makes sense to close the handbook with strategies for expanding this network of support, both formally and informally, within your school community. I'll begin with the most radical suggestion of all: reclaim the time and money allocated for your professional development.

SUPPORT BEYOND THE CLASSROOM: RECLAIMING PROFESSIONAL TIME

I sometimes wish an education researcher would do a study that verifies the direct correlation between the schedule of inservice days in schools and spikes in sales at local craft stores the week preceding these inservice events. I'm sure you could actually measure the duration of an education trend by the amount of crafts produced by teachers who had to sit through hours, even days, of presentations by outside experts hired by administrators. Cooperative learning has produced whole woolly sweaters and afghans that grace the home of many a teacher. By contrast, the remnants of the 1970s ITP reading instruction method are a few dusty macrame plant hangers. I suspect some teachers are cross-stitching their way through the outcomes and standards movement even as I peck these words.

I'm not knocking the professionalism of teachers. Our choices make good sense. Distar will come and Distar will go, but a needlepoint footstool is forever. As someone who has been involved in inservice work at all levels—as a presenter, an audience member, and part of an administrative team constructing a plan—I know firsthand that these programs don't work as they should. It isn't a lack of professionalism on the part of anyone involved. These programs are designed with the best of intentions, but the traditional structure and system of designing them doesn't fit the needs of the teachers they are supposed to serve.

What I have recommended that you do in this handbook will take time and money. You can go a long way on your own, using your own resources of time. Many good teachers have built their own personal development programs since the days of one-room schoolhouses. New money and pockets of time won't be easily found in schools. It's time to take a hard look at existing expenditures and the time in schools that are supposed to help teachers do their job in better ways. It's time to look at the potential of inservice days and budgets to assist teachers in becoming better observers and notetakers.

You may not be in a position to ask for what I am recommending—a reclaiming of your inservice days and the money your school administration has set aside to help you acquire skills. But I hope I can encourage some thinking about what money and time is available in your school for professional development and how you might be more active in making your needs known.

I've found that many schools do allow, even support, alternatives to the offered inservice event. But teachers aren't aware of these options, or the process of presenting an alternative and having it approved is so cumbersome that few attempt it. There is power in numbers. If you are considering reclaiming inservice time, it's essential that you're part of a group of teachers who agree to work together.

FINANCES

It's surprising how much money is spent for inservice presentations, even in tough times financially. Let's start with a modest budget, one for an outside presenter. Local districts where I live budget $600 a day for inservice presenters from outside the district, plus travel expenses. If you and your team had $700 to develop an alternative to the outside presenter, what could you do?

Sample Budget for Observation Workshop and Discussion Program

Roving Substitute Teachers $50 a day times 5 days = $250
Using a large chunk of your budget for roving substitutes would allow you and your colleagues to visit each other's classrooms, write observations, and compare notes on challenging students and challenging teaching situations.

Resource Library $150
Continued growth requires continued new reading. A collective library and budget for new titles allows everyone involved to share the same knowledge base and expands the conversation about options and alternatives far beyond your school walls.

Materials $200
You don't need much, as the "Tools of the Trade" section highlights. But you will need a variety of new supplies to encourage different ways of observing and writing about students.

Refreshments/Lunch $100
You should never underestimate the power of good food in fostering professional insights. It's worth the cost of a caterer, or the luxury of a lunch out, to allow your group to focus on discussions of your work in classrooms. And it's hard to stay mad at a colleague

who opposes your view of collaborative learning when you're dipping into the world's best Caesar salad.

There you have it—a modest $700 budget that can give you some of the essential elements you need to collaborate with your colleagues in new ways. And what could you do with the inservice day if there is no guest speaker to harangue, amuse, bore, or provoke you? You could:

- view videotape segments together and practice notetaking, comparing your notes;

- brainstorm different strategies for coding notes;

- work together to analyze one challenging child from each of your classrooms, based upon your notes and observations;

- develop new assessment strategies from your notes, and baseline expectations for teachers with notes;

- share what's working in your notetaking and what's not working;

- discuss ways to use your notes more effectively in collaborative school settings (i.e., consultations over special needs students, conferences with parents);

- discuss an article or chapter about assessment or notetaking, and apply these principles in your classroom;

- adapt or develop some notetaking forms to use consistently in different grade levels or across the entire school.

In short, you can use this time in whatever way will help you and your colleagues grow most professionally. Isn't that what inservice should be all about—days that serve our needs and the needs of our students?

Administrators know that many teachers have become cynical about inservice days. What they want and need are not complaints but plans that show how alternative uses of inservice time and money can support teacher development. Develop a plan that includes both a budget and clear details about how your work will move the goals of the school forward. Schools are perpetually working on improving their assessment systems and relations with parents. Good observational notes are a key tool for improvement in these areas. As you link your professional goals to those of the administration, you are more likely to find support for new approaches to inservice time.

Support Within the Classroom: Enlisting Colleagues, Visitors, and Students

One of my colleagues, fourth-grade teacher Marie Greve Krauss, has a large sign in her classroom that says, "Everyone learns here, including the teacher." You may want to institute a similar policy in your classroom: "Everyone takes notes here, including the teacher." One of the best ways to expand your base of observational notes on your students is to enlist students, colleagues, and visitors as notetakers. The more creative you are in thinking through how to enlist this support, the more perspectives you'll gain on your students and their work.

Many teachers require students to take notes throughout the day in a variety of logs. You might consider allowing students to respond in nontraditional ways to record behavior. In Clayton Holmes' sixth-grade classroom, students sometimes record the productivity and volume of their literature discussion groups through a series of bar graphs.

In Searsport, Maine, teachers have developed a procedure where everyone who enters a primary classroom is given a clipboard and told to write notes on each student. The clipboard contains a blank calendar for the month for each student, and the visitor is to write in an observation for that day for each child. This practice helps the teachers get new insights into the behaviors of their students. It also encourages the visitors to interact with the children and learn their names.

Many teachers swear by the value of "literacy digs," a concept developed by Denny Taylor (1993). This involves sifting through all the work of one child and notes with colleagues or parents. Just having a mountain of work laid out before you and working with others to compare that work to your notes leads to unexpected discoveries. These digs are particularly helpful when there is disagreement or confusion about the development of a child. Too often, these kinds of discussions take place with no real data to support statements. Literacy digs are also helpful in comparing your sense of a child through your notes with the actual work of the child. They are a good checkpoint for biases.

The benefits of having another pair of eyes to view your work and the behaviors of your students can't be overemphasized. One of the teachers I work with, Amanda Hersey, realized the same few children rarely appeared in her notes. She asked a few of her colleagues to observe and take notes on all of her students. When they compared notes, they saw that they all had the same set of three children who rarely, if ever, showed up in the notes. This shifted Amanda's thinking about her notetaking completely. She wrote, "What I thought was a personal deficiency, I now realize is a cultural issue. Obviously, certain behaviors trigger teachers' attention. Others don't. I talked about this with colleagues, around specific kids. What do we observe and why? How can we make sure we attend to the children who don't immediately capture our attention?" Enlisting colleagues to look at the same group of students will move you out of thinking about your strengths and deficiencies as a notetaker in isolation, and into considering the ways our culture and the social communities we work in view students.

It isn't easy to enlist colleagues and students to support your notetaking. And frankly, you might want to be a bit choosy about who you work with. Make sure you find someone who understands your goals and who you are as a teacher. Once you find that person or group, you'll wonder how you ever managed to go it alone.

Postscript

t's 8:00 P.M. and I'm anxious to go home. I've just finished working with twenty students, all teachers, in a graduate course. If I rush, I can tuck my daughter into bed and read her a quick story. But there is always one last thing I do before I leave.

I quickly scan the notes my students have kept on class that day and jot down a few of my own. I'm often surprised at the lukewarm response students had to an activity I thought would be engaging or the enthusiasm they have for what I thought would be a brief tangent to the focus of the evening's learning.

It's addictive. I can never leave without looking at my students' notes and writing a few of my own. It's become the basis of my growing confidence as a teacher and the way for me to put boundaries around my teaching life. Those few quiet minutes, scratching away in the classroom after the students have left, tie together the loose ends of everything I see and experience so quickly with students in every hour I spend with them. Fifteen minutes later, I drop all those notes off in the office and head out to my car.

I wish you the same good fortune in your observations and notetaking that I have found in mine. I hope you find the strategies in this book that will work for you and help you develop confidence in your ability to observe, assess, research, and develop a stimulating classroom. I hope this handbook simplifies, rather than complicates, your teaching life. And most of all, I hope in the coming weeks and months you discover some of the simple pleasures that come from observing your students closely and learning from the surprises those observations bring.

References

Austin, Terri. 1994. *Changing the View: Student-Led Parent Conferences.* Portsmouth, NH: Heinemann.

Ayers, William. 1993. *To Teach: The Journey of a Teacher.* New York: Teachers College Press.

Campbell, Kim. 1996. "You Can't Judge a Book by Its New Cover." In *Teacher Research: The Journal of Classroom Inquiry.* 3 (1), pp. 48–54.

Corsaro, William. 1981. "Entering the Child's World: Research Strategies for Field Entry and Data Collection in a Preschool Setting." In *Ethnography and Language in Educational Settings.* J. Green and C. Wallach, eds. Norwood, NJ: Ablex.

Daniels, Harvey. 1994. *Literature Circles: Voice and Choice in the Student-Centered Classroom.* York, ME: Stenhouse.

Heard, Georgia. 1989. *For the Good of the Earth and Sun.* Portsmouth, NH: Heinemann.

Stafford, Kim. 1991. "The Story That Saved Life." In *Stories Lives Tell: Narrative and Dialogue in Education.* Carol Witherall and Nel Noddings, eds. New York: Teachers College Press.

Taylor, Denny. 1993. *From the Child's Point of View.* Portsmouth, NH: Heinemann.

Annotated Bibliography

Austin, Terri. 1994. *Changing the View: Student-Led Parent Conferences.* Portsmouth, NH: Heinemann. *Excellent presentation from one sixth-grade classroom of how teacher, student, and parent observational notes can be woven together to create comprehensive evaluations of learning.*

Ayers, William. 1993. *To Teach: The Journey of a Teacher.* New York: Teachers College Press. *Very readable philosophical reflections of a teacher on his work with students. The second chapter is a detailed and thoughtful explanation of the practice and purposes of notetaking in his classroom.*

Baskwill, Jane, and Paulette Whitman. 1988. *Evaluation: Whole Language, Whole Child.* New York: Scholastic. *Short, readable text with many examples of children's and teachers' records. Lots of practical strategies.*

Cambourne, Brian, and Jan Turbill. 1994. *Responsive Evaluation.* Portsmouth, NH: Heinemann. *Includes a number of strategies for organizing notes and using question prompts to flesh out observations.*

Drummond, Mary Jane. 1994. *Learning to See: Assessment Through Observation.* York, ME: Stenhouse. *Emphasizes why close observation of students is essential in teaching. Rich in examples, it provides seamless integration of theory with practice.*

Goodman, Kenneth, Lois Bridges Bird, and Yetta Goodman. 1993. *The Whole Language Catalog: Supplement on Authentic Assessment.* Santa Rosa, CA: American School Publishers. *Chock-full of strategies, useful record forms, and additional resources.*

Hindley, Joanne. 1996. *In the Company of Children.* York, ME: Stenhouse. *Very thoughtful and practical examples of how third-grade teacher Joanne's notes inform her instruction. Especially strong in presenting children's notes, assessments, and written reflections.*

Hudson-Ross, Sally, Linda Miller Cleary, and Mara Casey. 1993. *Children's Voices: Children Talk About Literacy.* Portsmouth, NH: Heinemann. *The appendix on writing up student profiles from interview data has many helpful hints for interviewing students and building portraits of learners in their own words.*

Jasmine, Julia. 1992. *Portfolio Assessment for Your Whole Language Classroom.* Huntington Beach, CA: Teacher Created Materials. *Strength is many reproducible forms for record keeping—which can be easily adapted to your own needs and purposes.*

Kirby, Dan, and Carol Kuykendall. 1993. *Mind Matters: Teaching for Thinking.* Portsmouth, NH: Heinemann. *This book helps teachers and students put on the "lenses" of different kinds of thinkers—scientists, inventors, naturalists. An antidote to prescriptive "critical thinking" materials, the section on "thinking like an anthropologist" is especially relevant for writing better notes and observations. The suggested activities are useful for inservice or teacher development groups.*

Perrone, Vito. 1994. *Expanding Student Assessment.* Alexandria, VA: ASCD. *The sections that detail Patricia Carrini's techniques for observing, noting, and discussing students are particularly helpful.*

Reardon, S. Jeanne. 1991. "A Collage of Assessment and Evaluation from Primary Classrooms." In *Assessment and Evaluation in Whole Language Programs.* Bill Harp, ed. Norwood, MA: Christopher Gordon. *Excellent chapter that presents one teacher's evolution as an observer, notetaker, and evaluator of students. Rich in examples.*

Routman, Regie. 1991. *Invitations.* Portsmouth, NH: Heinemann. *In what's become the "bible" of literacy instruction strategies, there is a very helpful small section on records and notetaking strategies in the evaluation chapter.*

Taylor, Denny. 1993. *From the Child's Point of View.* Portsmouth, NH: Heinemann. *One of the best texts available that combines the political implications of teacher research and assessment with practical suggestions for implementing new observation strategies and collaborating with colleagues. Includes detailed accounts of how different teachers develop their own notetaking systems.*

Tierney, Robert J., Mark A. Carter, and Laura Desai. 1991. *Portfolio Assessment in the Reading-Writing Classroom.* Norwood, MA: Christopher Gordon. *Good introductory chapter on record keeping, easily adaptable to notetaking needs.*

ACKNOWLEDGMENTS

This project was inspired by the teachers in the 1995 University of Maine Summer Reading and Writing Literacy Camp. I thank these women—Mary Bagley, Julie Bishop, Kim Crosman, Jane Elwell, Debbie Folsom, Ruth Giangrande, Amanda Hersey, Kerri Little, Cherrie Mac-Innes, Karen Openshaw, Kathy Salkaln, Kim Skaves, Susan Ward, Mary-Ann Wheeler, Kimberley Wright, and Doreen Young—for their good humor and inspiration through a long, hot summer. Special thanks go to Associate Director Judith Bradshaw Brown, Team Advocates Jane Wellman-Little and Clayton Holmes, Research Associate Cynthia McCallister, and Site Assistant Janet Walker. They were cheerleaders, good friends, and great notetakers. Lois Bridges and Suzanne Drysdale provided extensive and helpful reviews of the book proposal. Diane DeMott Painter graciously came up with a title.

There would be no text without the many examples from teachers who so generously shared their best notetaking techniques and observation strategies with me. They are too numerous to name, but I hope they know how much I value their help.

Kelly Chandler provided incisive reading of drafts, and Jeff Wilhelm gave helpful suggestions for including secondary school examples. As always, the crew at Stenhouse—Philippa Stratton, Tom Seavey, Martha Drury, and Nicole DeSantis—provided just the right mix of prompt response and gentle prodding as deadlines loomed.

Ruth Shagoury Hubbard is my first, last, and best reader. I've lost track of where her ideas end and mine begin in what I write.

To all, my appreciation for making this little handbook far easier and more fun to put together than I imagined possible.